Reflect… through the Church's Year

Year B

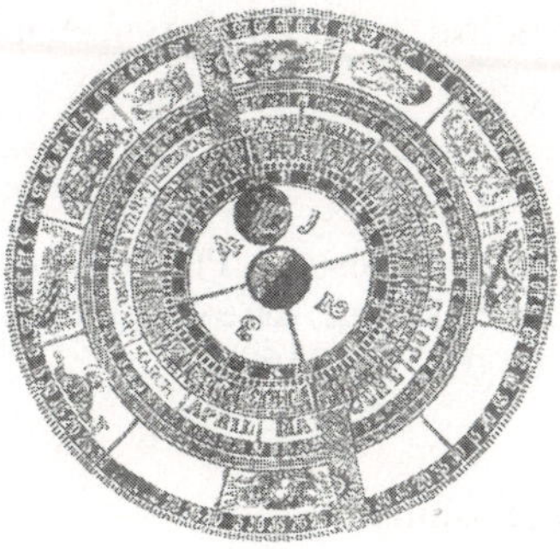

Michael Hollings

Prepared by Stephen Myers

McCRIMMONS
Great Wakering Essex England

The illustrations in this publication are taken from the book *Times & Seasons – Clip Art for the Liturgical Year* and published by McCrimmons. They are also available on computer disc in three volumes for DOS/Windows, Apple Macintosh and Acorn formats.

First published in 1995 by McCrimmon Publishing Co Ltd
10-12 High Street, Great Wakering, Essex SS3 0EQ.
Tel (01702) 218956 Fax (01702) 216082

ISBN 0 85597 571 7

Illustrations by Peter Edwards
Cover design by Nick Snode
Typeset in Times 11.5/13pt and 23pt Zapf International italic by Stephen Myers

Reprographics by Anagram Litho Ltd, Southend-on-Sea, Essex
Printed on 80gsm Bond
Printed by BPC Wheatons Ltd, Exeter

Contents

Introduction

THE WORD of God is alive and active. You and I, in any way God gives us, are committed to spreading the Word by our way of life, and through our speaking, teaching and love, the evidence of Christ-like service. It is easy to say this and to mean it! However, each one of us has to put this evangelising into practice.

The pages which follow form a part of my personal approach, which I will explain. I have no doubt from looking at the example of Jesus Christ that his life and presence were the most powerful instrument of his mission. He asked us to follow him taking up our cross each day. To me, Jesus Christ based his life on the will of his Father and was always in touch with him in prayer. We must follow him in prayer if we are to touch people.

Jesus also taught by word. Sometimes gently, sometimes sternly, sometimes forcibly. Priests, but also teachers of both sexes in schools, colleges, universities and the parish have a mandate to give air to the Word of God. The priest has the freedom of the pulpit, where what he is, how he prays, the simplicity of his approach all come together to make God's name known.

One of the aspects of this preaching I have tried to emphasise is that the Gospel needs opening up not only on a Sunday, but every day. So, whenever I have the control, I have always insisted that we should give a short few words of homily at EVERY MASS at EVERY WEEKDAY. There may only be a handful of people sharing the Eucharist, but they are the salt of the earth – and not only must this salt not lose its savour but it must have it enhanced.

So now I come to my final point. To back up the Readings, we have tried, not with unmixed success, to discuss them each Monday, when we have soup, cheese and bread at lunchtime. To follow them up and give something to take home, I have tried to write a 'lead' for our weekly newsletter. Apparently over time individuals have enjoyed them and found them worth praying over. As a result, it was decided to gather some together and publish them. I am grateful to Stephen Myers who has collated and edited them and also written and added a number where there were gaps among the originals. I hope you will find his efforts worthwhile and helpful to your own breaking open of the Word of God.

Michael Hollings
Feast of St John Mary Vianney
Curé of Ars

1st Sunday of Advent

Isaiah 63:16-17,64:1,3-8   1 Corinthians 1:3-9   Mark 13:33-37

Jesus points to the coming judgement of God, and so the call goes out: 'Stay awake!' But, it is a judgement of liberation - Isaiah expressed the great need of humanity. Saint Paul puts this in terms of the Christian life: the power of the Spirit enables us to stand firm.

MY DEAR Brothers and Sisters in Jesus Christ, Advent is a season of expectation. We are waiting and preparing for the coming of Our Lord, as if he had not already come to us nearly two thousand years ago. John the Baptist is our guide, and he says to us today what he preached during the first Advent: 'Prepare the ways of the Lord, straighten out his paths' (*Matthew 3:4*). We have to prepare for the coming of Our Lord into our lives by prayer and penance. In this way after each Christmas Day celebration we would be more committed to his service, and understand more fully how he wants us to live.

It is odd that so much about Christmas in our Society is about enjoying material things, food, drink and presents that make us richer. The riches which Our Lord wants to give us are quite different. The gifts which he brings will include a stronger faith in his Incarnation, that is, the truth that God became a man and dwelt amongst us. Another gift is a greater knowledge and trust in God's extraordinary love for each one of us, with the resulting joy and peace that this can bring. His gifts are given freely to us, but if we prepare for them we shall most certainly receive them in abundance. We receive and accept all good things as God's gifts given generously to us. We rejoice and say "thank you" to God. Christmas is a time to celebrate, but we have to remember that true Christmas riches are the spiritual ones, an increase of faith, hope and charity.

We should remember all those who cannot celebrate Christmas, either because they have no Church or priest, or because they have no food. If you sit and think about it, it is odd how so few people in the world can actually enjoy the good things that we have seen in our shops these last weeks. Think of the people in Ethiopia, in Chad, in Mali and several other African countries, for example. Starvation, suffering, misery are their daily companions. The thought should not give us the wrong kind of bad conscience. That would be an error. When you do these things for the poor and the suffering you do them to Christ himself. That brings its own reward. You become rich when you give. That is one of the secrets of Christmas.

2nd Sunday of Advent

Isaiah 40: 1-5, 9-11 2 Peter 3: 8-14 Mark 1: 1-8

The strange figure of John the Baptist is placed before us; yet he is the beginning of the 'Good News', the source of consolation for God's people, because his work prepares us for the work of Christ. The root of our consolation lies in the fact that God is faithful to his word and his promises.

ADVENT is the Church saying you have four weeks to prepare yourself, your family, friends and neighbours for celebrating of the Birth of Jesus Christ, Son of God and Son of Mary. We are preparing to welcome the *Light of The World* into the darkness of some aspects of our life - violence, marriage breakdown, lack of belief, fall-away in prayer and Mass-going, injustice, homelessness - the list goes on and on.

During Advent the daily and Sunday liturgies are full of hope - looking forward to the Incarnation - the coming of God in this world. In some ways, the atmosphere among people of today can be a bit hopeless, empty, without much vision of the future except in terms of gloom and disaster. Well, let us, as Christians, encourage each other to hope. This does not mean being overconfident, but refusing to be buried in gloom. Though Jesus Christ may seem a long way away - he has promised he is with us. He keeps this promise here and now today. Are we strong enough and simple enough to believe this?

There used to be - for all I know, there still is - a TV quiz programme called 'Mr. & Mrs.' The contestants were married couples; the wife would go into a soundproofed booth while the husband answered questions about her tastes and attitudes; then she would come out and her answers would be compared with his. The point is that, as we get to love people more, and hence to know them better, we are able to predict quite accurately how they will behave under certain circumstances - even if they have never yet experienced those circumstances. Likewise when we immerse ourselves in the love of God we begin to see him in our lives more and more. We do not lose hope and keep to the faith that has been given to us.

3rd Sunday of Advent

Isaiah 61:1-2,10-11 1 Thessalonians 5:16-24 John 1:6-8,19-28

The figure and mission of 'the One who is to come' becomes clearer as the Baptist gives witness to him. God's justice, his faithfulness to his own promises, is already at work; it will be as clear as day in Christ. For that reason, we of all people should know how to rejoice and be happy.

THERE IS a general call 'Seek the Lord'. Where do we look for the Lord here and now? Here are a few suggestions:

- *Seek the Lord in the world.* Today many find it difficult to see what God is doing in the chaos, the violence, and even the problems of global warming. Where is He? The only answer I know is not to write God off because of the chaos, but to look more deeply - look below the surface of chaos to the beauty.

- *Seek the Lord in your family,* friends, neighbours and neighbourhood. Here is a real challenge. To be close is beautiful, happy-making. But not easy! Sadly, the Christmas period which is supposed to be a time of peace and good will for all, often proves a time of irritation and even the surfacing of family problems and rows. In our own home let us make peace, joy and love - even when it is difficult. Pray for grace and strength if you know or feel that it will be a difficult time. To be close demands being open to the other person and we can be very private people. However, private or sharing - God is in each individual person and we must not just shut him in. It is of his nature to grow and to help others.

- *Seek the Lord in yourself.* We are told firmly - 'The kingdom of God is within you!' I have put these other two seekings first because the effectiveness of your seeking the Lord in the world or in your family depends on whether you have realised first, that essentially 'The kingdom of God is within you'. You and I must go inside ourselves to find the Lord - and that means prayer, deep prayer. Then care of your neighbours, relations and friends. If you go inside yourself to pray - if you are prepared to be silent in supplication to the Lord - well done.

- *Seek the Lord.* In the end, it is the Lord we seek who centres in our hearts. Meet him there as you can do if you can carve out even a tiny space of stillness, silence, peace in your probably busy day. Open your heart to him. Be still. Listen to the silence of his answer. His love is silent - reply to that love with patient and loving silence.

4th Sunday of Advent

2 Samuel 7: 1-5,8-11,16   Romans 16: 25-27   Luke 1: 26-38

Mary becomes, in a way that not even the prophets could have fully suspected, the 'House of God'. In faithfulness to his promises, God not only draws near to his people, he identifies himself with them. This Good News is given to us to be shared with everyone through our lives and example.

AS YOU read this, thank God for the wonder of his love. God so loved the world - that is he loved his creation of the universe, of this world with all it contains. He loved our ancestors down the ages. Today, he loves you with an everlasting love. This love - as the love of our own fathers and mothers - does not always seem very visible. We say 'if you love me, why do that to me? Why let this happen?' and so on. Love when it is real is very deep, and as St. Paul says 'love never comes to an end'. Sometimes we are happy in being able to feel loved, enfolded by love - human and divine. Sometimes we feel lonely and abandoned. Faith and trust and our love of God assures us - you are not alone: you are loved. Here is a lesson - the more you love, the more difficult and painful things may be! Christ's love led him to his suffering and death on the cross! But the more you love the more you will know deep down that you are loved: the more you will experience love.

In the hit musical *Les Misérables* there is a wonderful scene that shows the fruits of love. At the end of the show as the hero (Valjean) is dying all those he has loved and helped come to him and comfort him. Together they tell him that to:

Love another person is to see the face of God.

This is what we do when we share the love that we have received from Christ. So make this a feast of love by coming to Mass and Holy Communion, with your family and friends and neighbours. If you know anyone lonely or seemingly unloved, can you love them a little? If you cannot manage this yourself, tell someone. May *you* have a happy, peaceful, joyful and holy Christmas. Let us all wish each other the same.

Christmas Day

Isaiah 52:7-10 Hebrews 1:1-6 John 1:1-8

Jesus is the living Word of God, the Logos. He has been with the Father before time and now he has been born into time. He is the light of the world that will show us the way to be free.

The Lord said you are my son. This day have I begotten you.

EACH CHRISTMAS, we celebrate the feast by using the same readings. We do not change according to the normal cycle of the years 1, 2 or 3 (A, B, C). But there are three different masses given to us - Midnight, Dawn and During the Day. This means that though the message is the same all the time - that Jesus, Son of God, is born unto this world from the womb of the Virgin Mary, by the power of the Holy Spirit - the emphasis can be slightly different.

For me and for very many, there is a special mystery, awe and radiant joy about Midnight Mass. Normally the Church is beautifully decorated, music is interspersed with carols and Christmas songs, the crib, already prepared with loving care is blessed and opened, and hopefully everyone joins fully in the celebrations, not least in receiving Holy Communion.

This is the night when God gives us the amazing gift of his only Son. Surely it is only right and fitting that we should come with the poor but beautiful gift of ourselves. We should make his birth by receiving his gift to us of himself at the end of *His* life's journey *in* this world which begins at Christmas.

We should remember *in* all our joy and celebration that God's purpose in sending his Son as Christ into the world was to save us. Through his love he leads us through repentance and service of Him and our neighbours to the fullness of God's kingdom. The Kingdom of God is already here. When we come to mass we share in that Kingdom. The sad truth is that God's Kingdom has not yet been fully realised. We must understand that we are all on our own mission to make the Kingdom more real in our lives.

Christmas, then, is a wonderful time to show our generosity in opening ourselves to others, especially the poor, sick, forgotten in God's world. In loving us, he loves them, and asks us to respond to his love by loving others also. Alleluia.

The Holy Family

Ecclesiasticus 3:2-6;12-14 Colossians 3:12-21 Luke 2:22-40

Though we know little about the Holy Family we know that Jesus was raised in accordance to Jewish law and is the fulfilment of all the law asks. We should live our family life as Jesus would in compassion and kindness.

ONE OF the frustrations, but perhaps also the delights of the revelation that God has given to us is that it has many gaps in it. The frustration is that as human beings, we are naturally curious about what happened and where and when. We like to know about people and their families, lives and so on. Now we really know very little about the Holy Family, either individually or together. We know more about Jesus, little of Mary, even less of Joseph.

The delight, I think, is there for us in different ways. What happened to Mary and Joseph before Jesus was born is very important indeed and sets the whole tone and scene of the Gospel story. From Mary's 'yes' to God's messenger, through Joseph's faithfulness and humility, in the story of the visit to Elizabeth, we are given an insight into the characters introduced to us.

The Church, surely, does not want us to build imaginative stories about various happenings in their lives. If we want to do so we could go into the background of Palestine at the time of Christ, the history of Roman occupation, likely living conditions and so on. But this is only partially helpful. What we are asked to do is to meditate on what we are given and day by day to grow more deeply aware of the amazingly extraordinary fact of the incarnation, of God becoming a man. In which he asked the co-operation of his creation in the people of Joseph, Mary, Elizabeth and John the Baptist. This fact on its own is something wonderful to consider. God who is the beginning of everything needs the help of these people for his plan for our salvation to be realised. In his life he did not ignore their free will and simply asked.

Of Jesus and his humanity we can ponder endlessly. Without any more facts, the implications and outcomes go deeper and deeper into us with meditation and contemplation. Please give good space and time to God in prayer.

Mary Mother of God

Numbers 6:22-27 Galatians 4:4-7 Luke 2:16-21

Mary was able to see the fullness of her son's life and mission. Not only was she there to hear the story of the shepherds and the wise men but she was there at the foot of the cross and at Pentecost. She treasured all these things in her heart. It is through her actions that we are enabled to be freed from sin.

THIS FEAST of Mary is on 1st January- the end of the Octave of the Birth of Jesus. This feast is our opportunity after the concentration upon the wonder of God becoming man to centre on Mary. Motherhood is part of the amazing plan of God for his human creation (God bless all mothers). We know the story of her acceptance of motherhood from the message of the angel and the gift of the Holy Spirit. It reminds us how open and willing Mary was to give herself utterly to God's will. Her FIAT (be it done according to your will) was without any reservation.

I think one of the major problems that we all face is permanent commitment in our lives. This especially affects commitment in marriage and priestly and religious calling. Many people live together without binding vow to marriage. Many make marriage vows and then break up after only five years or even less. Not infrequently in teenage marriages, nullity is sought, a plea for such early vows is 'lack of due discretion'.

Now Mary pretty certainly was a teenager when she pledged herself. She was not then given an easy life. The pregnancy, birth, flight from Herod's terror, the early and later life were not what we might consider a satisfactorily stable condition. But her faithfulness, love, resort to prayer and her sharing with Joseph, together with her humble acceptance of living in the background, brought her through life into final death and glory. Meditate upon her faithfulness and how it reflects our own commitment.

2nd Sunday after Christmas

Eccesiasticus 24:1-2,8-12 Ephesians 1:3-6,15-18 John 1:1-18

The song of praise given to us by Simeon has become a song of the Church in its joy of having known that the Messiah has come and has redeemed us all. Jesus the light of the World has been born and has made us adopted children of the Father.

SOON AFTER the birth of Jesus, so the Gospel of Luke tells us, Mary and Joseph took Jesus to the Temple in Jerusalem. A very holy man, called Simeon, had been told by God that he would not die until he saw the Messiah. He was by then an old man, he had been waiting for many years. Prompted by the Holy Spirit he came to the Temple on this day and saw, a little baby. He instantly knew that all the years of waiting were now over, that the Messiah had come.

We have in Simeon a prime example of one committed to the power of prayer. He came to know, through prayer, that he would not die until he saw the Messiah, was told that he should go to the Temple, and once there was able to recognise the Messiah in a little child. In just the same way, when we pray for peace we come to understand better the nature of God's peace, we are told of the ways in which we ourselves are destructive of peace so that we can change, and we are shown the opportunities we have to promote and build peace.

Everything we think, say and do must be rooted in God. We communicate with God by means of prayer and that prayer leads through into action. That is the Christian dynamic and it can change the world. Peace is not something that has to be built by someone else; it has to be built by each one of us. We can have as much peace in the world as we want if we are prepared to pay the price and that price is our individual determination in seeking out what God wants of each of us and doing it.

Epiphany of the Lord

Isaiah 60:1-6   Ephesians 3: 2-3,5-6   Matthew 2:1-12

The Wise men stand for the wisdom of the time which was thought to be in the science of the stars and philosophy. Even this wisdom recognises that Jesus is the great King. They come from far to show that the message of the Lord is open to all people at all times. For all are part of the same body, Jesus Christ.

THE EPIPHANY is even more a mysterious piece of revelation than the coming of the shepherds to the stable. The origin, the coming, the star, the actual visit and the departure of the wise men are shrouded in a mist of questions on authenticity, mythology and meaning. In general the message is the message of the Saviour given to the shepherds of Israel and foretold in Israel's scriptures and at this point revealed to the Gentiles- to the rest of the world.

This is a very happy feast and in different places like Rome is especially a celebration for children, with an individual child chosen to represent Jesus for the day. In the past, it has been accepted as more important than Christmas itself, but in many ways Christmas is more widely celebrated.

As a general lesson, it is central to the teaching of Christ that, in the first instance he was sent, as he says himself, to those who are lost and coming from the tribes of Israel. However, the teaching gradually evolved in his own lifetime, until at the end before returning to his Father in Heaven, he tells his followers to go out to all nations. This is the mission now entrusted to all of us in our Baptism and Confirmation. It is not just priest or missionaries, but it is each and every Christian who Christ has commissioned to spread the word of God.

We should look at this personal mission and allow it to sink into us for it may be we do not yet feel our duty to the evangelisation, the giving of the Good News of Jesus Christ, as applicable to us. Yet it is applicable and should also be actual.

The Baptism of Our Lord

Isaiah 55: 1-11 1 John 5: 1-9 Mark 1: 6-11

By being baptised Jesus is sharing in our lives in the most intimate way possible. He shows us the way that we can become part of him. He takes on the totality of human nature so that he can redeem the totality of human nature. He shows he is the Messiah by his life. He shows he is the redeemer by his death.

WITH THE end of the Christmas season, which I hope we have all enjoyed and benefited from in our community, family and personal lives, we begin the Sundays of Ordinary Time. Their number varies, according to the date of the beginning of Lent. After Pentecost they are taken up again and go on till the end of the Church's year and the beginning of Ordinary Time.

In fact, the first Sunday is the celebration of the Baptism of Christ and we can meditate on this remarkable happening. We all know a bit about the Sacrament of Baptism and how it brings us into the life of Christ - a new spiritual life in him.

Why did Jesus need to be bapised? It was a wonderful example of the humility of both Jesus and John. It was also a mutual acceptance of each other and the very different roles which God had given them in His plan of salvation. John had a very lonely role - the voice crying in the wilderness. Not himself as the Messiah but calling for repentance and preparing for the one to come, Jesus. And now Jesus has come and John sees him authenticated in the presence of the Spirit as dove descending on Jesus and the voice from heaven saying 'This is my Son.' (*John 3:13-17*)

In the Baptism of Jesus, he goes down into the waters of the Jordan not to have his sins taken away, but rather symbolically to take on all the sins of the world mirrored in the Jordan waters. After this, like the scapegoat driven in olden days from the camp into the desert bearing the sins of all the people, Jesus himself is driven into the desert by the Spirit. Here there is such an amount to ponder on. Let us try to start the ordinary year by an assessment of what our Baptism means in our lives.

2nd Sunday of the Year

Samuel 3:3-10,19 1 Corinthians 6:13-15,17-20 John 1:35-42

God calls us by name, are we prepared to receive him? When we draw near to the Lord we understand more fully our mission, to live as part of Christ's body (as St. Paul reminds us). John the Baptist, the bridge between the Old and New Testament, guides us to recognise Jesus as the Christ. Like the disciples we must recognise him, follow him and remain in him.

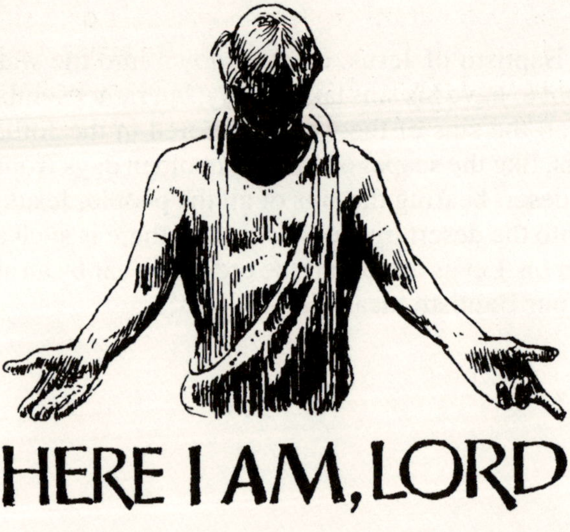

THE FIRST reading and the Gospel this week presents us with two different calls from God - Samuel in the Old Testament, John and Andrew in the New. Well, God has told us that he knows each of us by name, but recognition of the voice of God or his call seems often to be less easy than we might hope. With Samuel it is Eli, the prophet, who puts him right and assures him that he must answer the voice directly and not come running to Eli. With John and Andrew, it is John the Baptist, whose disciples they were, who actually draws their attention to Jesus. These two stories underpin the importance of each of us having someone to turn to in perplexity or doubt, when a difficult decision is called for, when there seems to be no solution, no way backwards or forwards - just a sense of being lost, a fear, a terrible indecision. This does not have to be a trained counsellor or therapist. It can be one of the family, a close friend, doctor, priest and so on. Just ponder on whether you have such a person in your life.

This weekend is also a time for each of us to say clearly to God: 'Here *I* am, Lord' putting the emphasis on *I*. I seldom meet a person who at one time or another does not feel alone, forgotten by God, or even cut off from God by one's own sin and self-imposed distancing. Do not be misled. We may have gone blind or deaf, but God always listens, always hears and never ceases from loving you, however far away you may seem from each other.

3rd Sunday of the Year

Jonah 3:1-5,10   1 Corinthians 7:29-31   Mark 1:14-20

God's love and grace has no boundaries or limits as can be seen in the sending of Jonah to Nineveh, a pagan city, and its conversion. Jesus shows that we must go beyond conversion. He demands that we show the faith that we have by repentance and belief in the Good News.

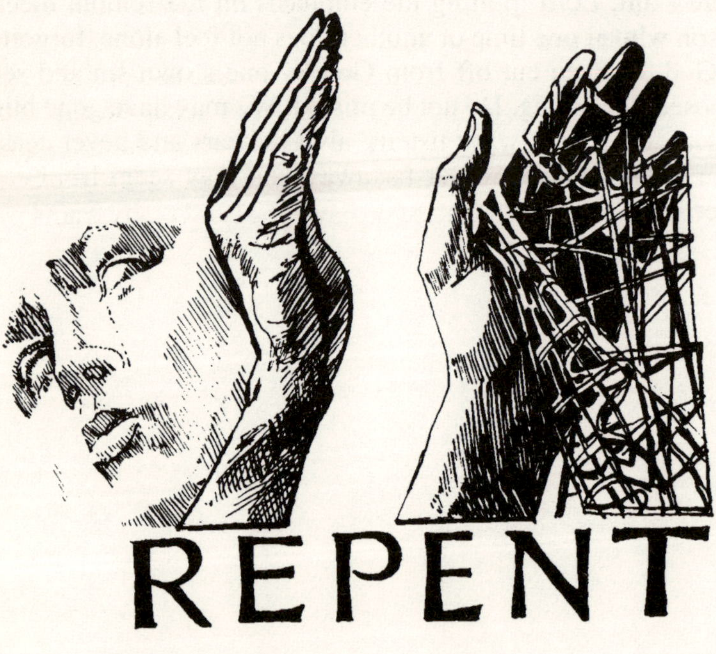

EACH ONE of us, as we come to Church, come for some reason. This reason is personal, but it has a common origin - belief or attempt to believe in Jesus Christ - Son of God and son of Mary.

Perhaps in our own way we are responding to the call of Jesus in today's gospel to repent, believe in the Good News and follow him. We follow him when we do as he asks us. We show our faith in the Good News when we receive him in word and sacrament. We repent when we dedicate ourselves to him through the sacraments.

For most of us, we also have a common origin in baptism. Through this Sacrament we each and all become members of the Body of Christ. We are temples of the Holy Spirit - Jesus, as he promised, is with us always. For God to share our human condition is astounding - unbelievable, but you and I do believe. So - if we believe - are we prepared to give ourselves in our belief to the commands of Jesus? I ask this because, despite very regular and even frequent words of encouragement, there are a large number of people who do not 'take and eat - take and drink'. Jesus gave this direct command; why do some not take and eat? You must answer that if you do not take and eat. If there is anything on your conscience which prevents you - please, please talk to someone about any difficulty you have; the Lord really wants you at his table. Come!

4th Sunday of The Year

Deuteronomy 18:15-20   1 Corinthians 7:32-35   Mark 1:21-28

Jesus is the new Moses predicted in the first reading. He is more than just one of the prophets, He is God's Son, the Word of God. His words have authority and speak to us at every level. We should recognise that he is the Holy One of God and, like Paul, make ourselves ready to receive him.

THERE IS an old Scottish story about a man who died and went to meet the judgement of God. He pleaded ignorance saying: 'I dinna ken' and the reply he got from God was: 'Ye ken noo!' For us, when we come to be judged, the plea of ignorance will not be enough.

This Sunday gives us both Old and New Testament illustrations of the kind of authoritative teaching which has come to us through revelation and is still coming through the scriptures and the thinking of the Church. Moses who was a really tough leader, prophet and teacher nevertheless had great difficulties with the children of Israel who did a lot of complaining, bickering and backbiting. No matter how hard he taught them, no matter how clearly he passed on the revelation and law from God, almost as soon as his back was turned, the people made and worshipped man-made idols. This reading promises another prophet like Moses sent by God to receive and utter God's commands, Jesus. I'm sure we all know they fell away again later.

When Jesus Christ came, as today's Gospel tells us (*Mark 1:21-28*), the people in the synagogue saw him cast out a devil and teach a new teaching and with authority. Yet many questioned or refused that authoritative teaching. We think that these people were foolish beyond imagination but we are no better.

Today the kind of question we should put to ourselves is our reaction both to Scripture and to the teaching of the Church. The climate of many scholars and of others is to question the authority of scripture. Some dismiss completely, some in part, some are indifferent, some contemptuous of the scriptures. The Church's teachings can suffer the same fate, even at times among those who say they are Catholic.

How then do you and I react - what is our attitude, our acceptance, our love and our prayerful listening? We all still have much to learn. Or do we feel that we have all the answers? Such arrogance is only the folly before the fall. We do not have all the answers. It is right to bring our gifts of intellect and thought to scripture and tradition but we must also bring our prayer so that we can hear the Lord speaking to us in our faith, guiding us and loving us.

5th Sunday of the Year

Job 7:1-4, 6-7   1 Corinthians 9:16-19, 22-23   Mark 1:29-39

We are children of God who should put our faith in him. Like Job our prayer should be a cry of faith and complete confidence in our loving Lord. Like Paul we should look for no return from this faith other than to have a share in His life. Jesus, the healer, wanted his message to be shared with all so that he might be recognised as the Messiah.

THERE IS no more emphatic writer and preacher than St. Paul. In writing to the Corinthians some of which forms today's second reading, he puts very strongly that the duty of preaching the Gospel has been put on him, not chosen by him. His reward is not a cash reward, but it is in being able to offer the good news freely. Interestingly, he goes on to write that free as he is, he has made himself a slave of everyone. I am sure each of us has met the sort of person who slaves away so hard that burnout comes or we may even be such a person ourselves. I certainly know priests, sisters and many good and devoted people like teachers who never seem to rest. I feel that sometimes some of us are so busy doing God's work, we have no time for God.

It is a very serious error we can get into when we take everything on, are bad at delegating and feel guilty if we are relaxing or caring for ourselves and having a holiday. Hard as we may work, overwhelming as the load may be, time for ourselves and time for God is essential. Christ gives us such a wonderful example in this Sunday's Gospel (*Mark 1: 29-39*). There is a vivid description of Jesus curing Simon's mother-in-law, spending the whole evening curing and healing those who came crowding in from the town. And then the important passage I want to underline for each of us:

> *In the morning, long before dawn, he got up and left the house and went off to a lonely place and prayed there.*

To be able to have time to pray must have been important for Jesus as we read that he did this again and again. In this gospel reading it even seems as if he left people behind so that he could pray. As always, Jesus, our example, is showing us what we must do in our lives.

Paul says it is his duty to preach the Gospel. It is true to say that it is ours as well. But another of our duties is to look after ourselves in such a way that we have the time to meditate on the Gospel, to be alert and good-tempered, not permanently at a stretch, irritable and without time for people. Unfortunately, it is quite easy to get like that - and it is really of value neither to God nor humanity.

6th Sunday of the Year

Leviticus 13:1-2,44-46 1 Corinthians 10:31-11:1 Mark 1:40-45

In love and charity Jesus touched the leper. His kindness led him to break what had become a religious as well as a social ban. Through their failure to recognise Jesus as the Messiah and their lack of charity the people in turn made him an outcast. It is the need for us to have charity as our guide that leads Paul to call on the people of Corinth to be helpful to all.

YEARS AGO, I was involved in a leper colony in South India and once I had the privilege of going there, staying with the wonderful Belgian woman who had founded it, joined with the lepers, seeing them at work and play, and making friends with them. Things are very different in the world now from the time when Jesus lived. Though, I believe, sadly leprosy is still spreading, even though there is more medical help, more knowledge and a greater possibility of helping without becoming a *pariah* catching the awful disease. The Gospel today shows us how far Jesus was prepared to go in helping those in misfortune. It also shows how an incautious tongue, yesterday or today can cause real hardship.

When asked by a leper to heal him, Jesus took pity on him, stretched out his hand, touched him and healed him immediately. That is the beautiful, self-giving witness of Jesus who came for those outcasts. He knew the Leviticus instruction which is today's first reading (*Leviticus 13:44*). The leper is unclean. He must live outside the camp. Yet Jesus touched him. Aware of the danger of the news spreading, he sternly ordered the man not to talk about the cure - but he did ! And so Jesus had to avoid going to towns and had to stay outside in places where nobody lived.

What a lesson ! How far are we prepared to go in becoming pariahs, despised, shunned because of our views or way of life or association with ne'er-do-wells? For example would you be willing to shake the hand of someone who you knew was HIV positive or who had full blown AIDS? Would you be able to overcome your own prejudice and help those in need? And on the other tack, do we sufficiently guard our tongues or are we liable to gossip, tittle-tattle or even take away people's characters. Jesus challenges us here - let us take up that challenge ourselves.

7th Sunday of the Year

Isaiah 43:18-19,21-25 1 Corinthians 1:18-22 Mark 2:1-12

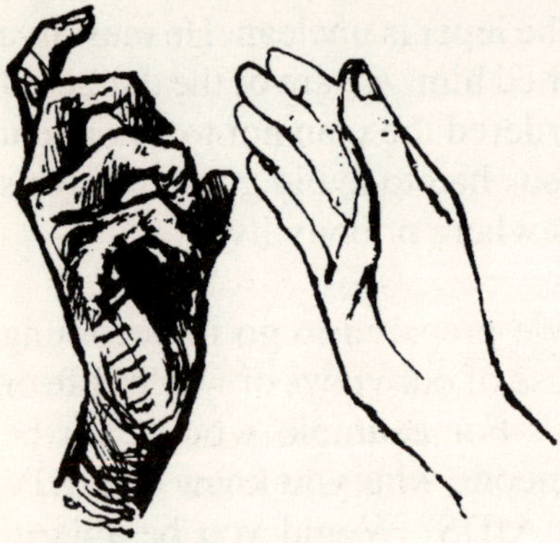

Isaiah tells us that it is the Lord who forgives sins, yet Jesus claims that authority. Through their incomprehension the Scribes accuse him of blasphemy. He asserts his position and shows them the error of theirs. Paul tells us that it is through Christ that we find the authority of God active in our lives.

'I CAN'T believe I am forgiven! I know you say I am and that I should forget the past and go on feeling free and not guilty. But I do feel guilty and I do not feel forgiven.' This was said to me recently. It is not the first time. It is hardly likely to be the last. To me it is one of the major problems I have to face in quite a large number of people. What is wrong? Why do they feel this way? Is there something wrong with the sacrament of Reconciliation in the Church or is there something wrong with them?

Periodically, the Church in her wisdom brings into the Sunday readings the teaching of Jesus and the forgiveness of sins. That is so this Sunday when we find Jesus facing a paralytic whose friends were so determined to get him to Jesus inside a house that they actually stripped off the roof and let him down from above the heads of the crowd within.

Jesus places the emphasis on faith and immediately says: 'My child, your sins are forgiven.' (*Mark 2:1-12*). It does not seem to have much to do with curing the paralytic, but some of the scribes got uptight at Christ saying 'Your sins are forgiven' because only God can forgive sins. Jesus' reply was to say he would prove he had power to forgive sin by telling the paralytic to take up his bed and walk - which he did. Part of the problem may be the difficulty that we have in 'letting go' of our sinful self. We hang on to our sins and so push the love of God further away from ourselves. Jesus has redeemed us and through him we are all forgiven. But still we must receive that forgiveness.

Now, for those who doubt that their sins are forgiven, here is a salutary lesson. God can and does forgive sin and this is reiterated time and again in the Scripture. What is very relevant here for those I mentioned at the beginning of this little piece is that Jesus ties *Faith* very tightly to forgiveness. I'm afraid it may be that those who doubt that God forgives them are lacking faith. Think long and hard about this if you feel unforgiven. Your prayer should be from another part of the Gospel where a person calls out to Jesus

'Lord, I believe, please help my unbelief'.

May God's spirit guide you more deeply into believing that with God all things are possible - even forgiveness of your sins.

Ash Wednesday

Joel 2:12-18   2 Corinthians 5:20-6:2   Matthew 6:1-6,16-18

To serve the Father is an end in itself. We do not need to boast about it, we do not need the praise of others because we do it. Why? Because of love of the Father. All we should want is to follow his wish for us. What more do we need?

WHAT IS Ash Wednesday going to mean to me and to you?

The ashes are blessed at each Mass. The symbol of ash placed on the forehead of each one of us. It reminds us that we are human, and that we have a beginning and an end on earth. It reminds us that as human beings we are weak as well as strong. We have faults, we fail as well as succeeding. Jesus came to open the eyes of the poor, giving them the good news of salvation. He began his message by saying: 'Repent and believe the Gospel' (*Mark 1:15*). *Ashes remind us of repentance.*

This is a season when we are asked to remember this repentance and bring it to the front of our minds. This means eating less or eating nothing! Jesus, whose 40 days in the desert we follow in Lent's 40 days, fasted in the desert. Today more people fast for health reasons or for the look of their figure than fast for spiritual reasons - growing closer to God. Wait a moment though! Many people join in with fast days for the Third World, for CAFOD and others. At Medjugorje, the message of fasting is strong. Well then - what about fasting (at least to some degree) each week in Lent? Try to decide on Friday - do it singly, or do it as a family. Link it with deliberately saving something from food, drink, sweets, cigarettes and so on. - and giving that to CAFOD.

Something extra for Lent? There are many things we can do to make Lent a special time.

- An extra Mass each week (some will go every day, I know).

- The Stations of the Cross by yourself - or with the others.

- Join one of the prayer/Scripture groups, or one of the ecumenical groups in your area.

- Give a little extra time to your personal prayer.

What ever you do make sure that this Lent is a special time of preparation for the wonderful time of Holy Week and Easter. When we move through the remembrance of the last days of Jesus to his death and resurrection. This is a wonderful season because of what is at the end of it.

1st Sunday of Lent

Genesis 9: 8-15   1 Peter 3: 18-22   Mark 1: 12-15

The temptation of Jesus in the wilderness. While Mark does not dwell on this episode, he links it very closely with the beginning of Jesus' preaching ministry. The will of his Father takes precedence over everything else in Jesus' life. Like Noah, we are saved by the waters, in this case of baptism, which identify us with Christ. So, the Father's will must be our guide in life.

AS THE whole period of Lent forms a final preparation for those who are called catechumens - people approaching Baptism who are not infants - the readings are there to lead, guide and enlighten them. We who are already members of the Church are reminded of our need to repent and follow the Gospel. So now we have a chance to make the following of the Gospel a reality through the liturgy of Lent. We are all going forward towards the re-enactment in Holy Week of the new and eternal covenant of Jesus Christ. So it is fitting that our first reading this Sunday is all about Noah and the original Covenant made by God with him.

Set my bow in the clouds and it shall be a sign of the covenant between me and the earth.

This begins a series of covenants and promises by God to his people and of course they culminate at the death and resurrection of Jesus.

I'm not sure whether the idea of making Lenten resolutions has any sense of origin in God's covenant. At any rate, it has been a custom over the centuries for individuals to make such resolutions. They can be good, they can perish along the weeks and make us feel guilty. The Church gives us a suggestion in the three eminent good works - prayer, fasting and alms giving. Why not resolve to follow that pattern. All of us can do well to emphasise prayer and to develop our habit of giving time to God each day. Much of fasting has gone by the board, but CAFOD always has one Family Fast Day in Lent and we might extend that to each Friday. We can also link that with trying to give some money saved from food and drink towards the poor, homeless, refugees and dispossessed. Try any little Lenten extra - only be sure not to give up half way through.

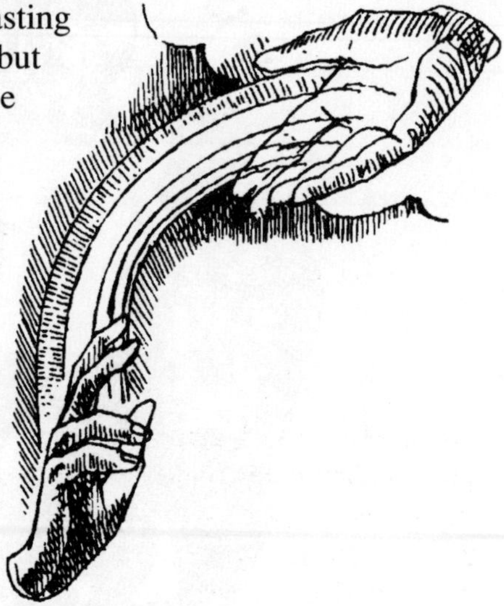

2nd Sunday of Lent

Genesis 22:1-2,9-13,15-18 Romans 8:31-34 Mark 9:2-10

The Transfiguration of Jesus on the mountain. Already the shadow of the cross looms large; for our salvation God will spare not even his own Son. Also, he will ask of us sacrifice just as he asked it of Abraham. This is the mystery of the Son of Man in practice; we are to learn of it like the apostles - the hard way.

YOU COULD say that this Sunday takes us a few steps closer to the cost of God's covenant with us. Cost like that of Abraham going along with God's demand that he sacrifices his only son, Isaac. This can be seen as a foretaste of God's offering of his only son to fulfil the later covenant. For Abraham, the covenant promise for the future was a result of his obedience even to accepting the death of his son. In Christ it is in following his Father's will that he became obedient even to death on the Cross (Paul to the Philippians). This means that the New Covenant that Jesus talked of at this Last Supper will also be fulfilled.

The story of the Transfiguration of Jesus on the mountain forms an important bridge between the Old and the New Testaments. The bridge can be seen in the two figures with Jesus. Moses who represents the covenant of the Law and Elijah who represents all the prophets and their foretelling of the Christ. That person is the third party Jesus whom they have joined on the mount.

This gospel is also a reminder of the content and cost of transfiguration, though it is not stated in Mark's version. Elsewhere the vision includes the reference to the conversation Moses and Elijah were having about his passing which would take place in Jerusalem. From this we can grasp that the glory is all mingled with the pain and suffering of his passion and death. It reminds me of the joyful acceptance and recognition of the recently born Jesus in the Temple by Simeon and at the same time him telling Mary that a sword would pierce her heart.

The mixture of pain and joy in love is ever present in our own lives too. It may be helpful for us to realise that what ever pain and suffering we go through in our lives Jesus understands. He has suffered, has been happy, has been lonely, has been beaten, has gone through a painful death. In short we have a saviour who has shared our human condition and is therefore much closer to us than we realise.

3rd Sunday of Lent

Exodus 20: 1-7   1 Corinthians 1: 22-25   John 2: 13-25

Jesus, the New Temple of God. He replaces the Law given by God to Moses, which is not destroyed, but taken up into the true worship 'in the spirit and truth'. Christ asks for faith above all else, a faith which is deep and personal, because he is the 'power and wisdom of God'. Baptism is only the beginning of our response in faith.

THIS WEEK we have the Old Testament reading from Exodus on the ten commandments. The two great commandments are commandments of love - 'love God, love your neighbour as yourself'. The ten commandments merely emphasise these two.

Commandments one to three are on relationships with God, the rest are on relationships with our neighbour. God's covenant and God's law are both expressions of his love. If we accept his law and his love our lives are changed and we prove our love for him by keeping his law. Later Jesus says, 'If you love me, keep my commandments'.

Forgiveness. This is a whole area of love for us. Shown in God's patience with those who broke his commandments. Often it is only through forgiveness that we can move forward into reconciliation and peace. An 'armed truce' or a 'ceasefire' is not enough. Please tackle this area of forgiveness in your own life - and spread it to your neighbourhood. This takes humility, patience and forgiveness. Try!

Peace. God's covenant of love is the gateway to peace. It must also be the solid foundation of peace. You and I must pledge ourselves to be positive in working for justice and peace. There are many other parts of the world, Northern Ireland, parts of Russia, Tibet, China, India and Pakistan, Thailand, where there is no peace. Pray, pray, pray.

4th Sunday of Lent

2 Chronicles 36:14-16,19-23 Ephesians 2: 4-10 John 3: 14-21

Jesus, the Source of Eternal Life. The 'lifting up' of the Son of Man on the cross is destined for the salvation of everyone. Just as God has saved his people in the past, he continues to do so through his Son. Our response of faith, therefore, demands that we live 'the good life as from the beginning he meant us to live it'.

OFTEN, RIGHT in the middle of Lent we have Mothering Sunday because of the ancient entrance antiphon: 'Rejoice, Jerusalem...you will find contentment at her consoling breasts.' Jerusalem seen as our mother became symbol of all mothers. Let us rejoice in and for Mothers today.

Jerusalem suffered many hardships in her history as she does today. So too Holy Mother Church and our own mothers often have much to suffer in the modern world situation. But Jesus points us through his words to Nicodemus that

> *God sent his son into the world, not to condemn the world, but that through him the world might be saved.*

You and I are part of a world which is being saved all the time. And the Lenten season is one of our chances to be enlightened.

There is an oldish saying 'If you are not part of the solution, you are part of the problem.' Jesus is more forthright. He says: 'Anyone who is not *for* me is *against* me.' Just to be indifferent is not enough. The Gospel reading goes on to say that 'though the light has come into the world, men have shown they prefer darkness to light'.

Our approaching entrance to the season of the Passion gives us a further reason and opportunity for examining ourselves and our attitudes to make sure our Lenten resolve holds firm and is

strengthening. The way we come, mind and heart, to Holy Week will determine what we put into and what we get out of this holiest of seasons. If we have been slack during Lent it is not too late to try harder now. If we have been trying, by God's grace, let us keep up our efforts. God will give the increase.

5th Sunday of Lent

Jeremiah 31: 31-34   Hebrews 5: 7-9   John 12: 20-33

Jesus the centre of unity for the whole family of God. Face to face with the 'hour' of his passion. Jesus does not shrink, but carries out the will of his Father - this is why he is glorified; his death is the means whereby God reaps for himself a universal harvest. In him, God has made a new covenant with the human race, and so he is the 'source of eternal life and salvation for all who obey him' in faith.

ON THE very threshold of the Passion, we are taken back once again to a prophecy of Jeremiah (*Jeremiah 31:31-34*) in which God promises a new covenant, not an earlier one where God took the people from Egypt which the people broke. Now the promise is:

> *Deep within them I will plant my law, writing it on their hearts.*

It is good to reflect again on the use of *heart* on which the Law is to be written. This should help us to realise that God's covenant and his law is for the whole person - body, mind, heart, soul - we are to be living embodiments of God's gift to us.

But the second reading which is taken from the Hebrews keeps in front of us the close relation of suffering and love. We are told of Christ going through the torment of facing death and offering up prayer and entreaty, aloud in silent tears. It then says strangely that: 'he submitted so humbly that his prayer was heard.' It is difficult for us to see how it was heard except that 'he learnt to obey through suffering'. So we too must learn to obey through suffering on our way to death and eternal life.

In the Gospel, Christ tells us that a grain of wheat has to fall to the ground and die in order to produce a rich harvest. This Jesus himself did and he has left us an example, that we follow in his steps.

Palm (Passion) Sunday

The final phase of Our Lord's ministry begins; the triumphant entry into Jerusalem underlines the true nature of his messiahship, in humility and service. Just how far that humility and service must go is pointed out by the reference to the Servant of God - no matter what the cost, the will of God must be done. The passion according to Mark in all its detail and brutality confronts us with the ultimate stage in the mystery of the Son of Man. But in his death is his glory and the centre of our profession of faith.

THIS WEEKEND - Palm Sunday - we witness Christ's triumphal entry into Jerusalem, with shouts of Hosanna and acclamation from the crowd. In the minds and hearts of the crowd this was the beginning of restoring the worldly power of the kingdom of Israel, oppressed as the kingdom was by the occupying forces of

Rome. Jesus rejects this and goes off out of the city to stay with friends and then teaches daily in the Temple until the time of the Last Supper and his arrest comes. In this world, the whole thrust and push and educational drive is supposed to be towards achievement and success. As Christians there is a very real dilemma here - are we not meant to use our talents, to work for success, power?

By sharing the experience of hearing the triumphal entry and Christ's rejection of that worldly conquest, our own worldly aims and ambitions are given a different colouring. By sharing the reading of the Passion story, the awfulness, the horror of the cruelty of those created out of God's love is highlighted. We can draw on these scenes when we pray, against the horror of violence and cruelty in today's world. We can ponder, also, the injustice of Christ's condemnation in relation to the failure and lack of justice so widely spread around the world at this time.

On Maundy Thursday, we enter into Christ's loving service and self-giving both in the washing of the feet and in the celebration of the Lord's Supper. Here we have Jesus' two great acts of love; he washes the feet of his disciples in humility and service, urging them to follow his example, and then he anticipates his own death by giving bread and wine to his disciples saying 'this is my body' and 'this is the cup of my blood'.

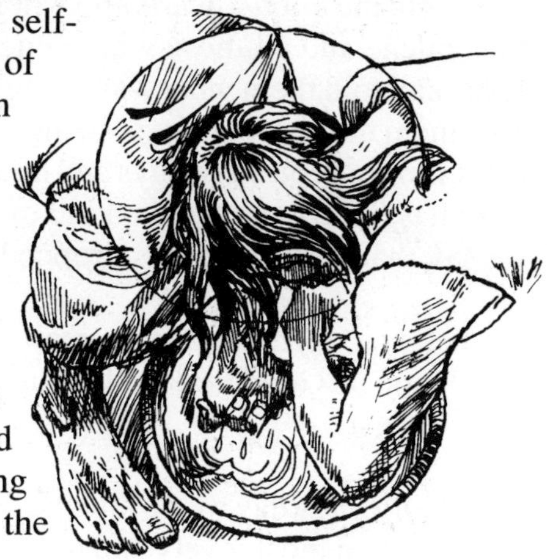

There is so much depth, beauty and love in this celebration, everyone should do their very best to join the community of love and receive his gift of himself in Holy Communion. Please respond to his call.

Good Friday provides the opportunity for us to centre on the Cross. The solemnity and sadness should be as tangible to us as it is when we are bereaved - it should go really deep into our consciousness and our unconscious. This should be truly a day of prayer, fasting, and giving alms in communion with the sorrowfully beautiful celebration. There are many ways of meditating on the meaning of Good Friday for us. I want this time to meditate on the Cross, for it is the Cross which we acknowledge and venerate in a central way during the afternoon liturgy.

On this day of all days and at this time, it takes little imagination to picture the sense of abandonment, horror, pain, fear and almost despair in the minds, hearts and whole being of Mary, John, Mary Magdalene and all those who witnessed Jesus' death. Although Jesus had told them what was going to happen, it did not seem to give them the consolation of being able to say to each other 'Yes, but it is only to be three days and he will rise again.' I expect each of us has experienced some kind of desolation in our lives when we say that the bottom has dropped out of our world.

I believe, then, that it is really vital for us to experience desolation on Good Friday - feeling that emptiness of life without Jesus Christ.

On Holy Saturday we go into the darkness to emerge in the light of Christ in a most lovely and moving celebration. You must not miss this. It is a wonderful occasion for our personal and collective renewal in Christ. On this night, also, we shall have the joy of welcoming new members to our parish community. I would like to highlight two parts of this wonderful liturgy, that of Baptism and the Eucharist.

Baptism. First and foremost this is our Christian family celebration. This Saturday is the night set aside for bringing to the new life of Baptism in Christ, those who have not before been members of his body, the Church. It is also during this night and Easter Day that we individually renew the promises of our own baptism probably made for us at the time by our parents and Godparents. These promises are summed up in the first one, 'Do you reject sin so as to live in the freedom of God's people?' Each of us is asked to answer 'I do'. So let us make those promises our own in daily life - building up the life of the Spirit by living the 'sacrament of the present moment', in our ordinary daily round. Thus, with nothing extraordinary at all you can show to others what an old friend of mine called 'the daily miracle of holy life'.

Eucharist. The fruit of the Passion, death and resurrection of Jesus is for our daily comfort and strength - the body and blood of Jesus Christ in Holy Communion. Our Easter Communion is a celebration of great joy. We enter into Christ and he enters into us, so that we become more united than ever at our baptism, because this mysterious presence of the Lord fills us with his love. Eucharist, as you know, means thanksgiving. With all this blessing from God, we are churlish indeed, if we are not full of thanksgiving for all God's mercy and love. As we enjoy this new spring, our reaction will be best and most beautiful if we fully enter into covenant with God who has given us the new and everlasting covenant of his love. Alleluia!

Easter Day

Acts 10: 34, 37-43   Colossians 3: 1-4   John 20: 1-9

'Seeing is believing'; the witness of the apostolic group to the resurrection of Jesus. This witness we are invited to rely on and to share ourselves. Then we begin the process by which newness of life becomes a reality for us just as it did for the apostles. Forgiveness of sins through faith in Jesus Christ - this is the message of the Church for our age too, to be preached 'in sincerity and in truth'.

WE KNOW there are so many horrors throughout the world. Let us hope that they will not be made worse over the Easter period. Let us more positively hope and pray that there may be greater peace, more joy, more prayer, so that God's human race may allow him more opportunity to work out his will through us. We surely have to go through Holy Week to come to Easter. Our Passion, our Holy Week, is the living of life here day by day. This is the common plan for all people. It varies - some live a short time, some a long time - some seem to have a huge dose of pain - some seem to have very little. Well - what each of us should do is to start where we are and live from there. So, in the yearly calendar, we have come through to Easter - with all its joy. Please enjoy it! And this will mean joining the central point of the festival - Jesus Christ risen from the dead. Alleluia! This is the day the Lord has made. Alleluia!

2nd Sunday of Easter

Acts 4: 32-35 1 John 5: 1-6 John 20: 19-31

The image of the primitive Christian community 'united heart and soul' is placed alongside the profession of faith of Thomas; just as that community shared a resurrection faith, so do we. This faith can overcome the 'world', because it is brought into being and fostered by the power of the Spirit of God himself.

THERE IS so much talk about the freedom of the individual nowadays, that talk about "obedience" and "following God's will" may almost be considered old fashioned. Yet, if we look at Christ himself what do we see? He is the example of obedience: "I am not trying to do what I want, but only what he who sent me wants" *(John 5:30)*. The thing that we have to realise, however, is that it was not a matter of following laws and commandments. Christ did what he did out of love: "The world must know that I love the Father; that is why I do everything as he commands me" *(John 14:31)*. Christ and the Father are one in love: "Believe me when I say that I am in the Father and the Father is in me" *(John 14:11)*. What, then, does Christ expect from us? "If you obey my commands, you will remain in my love, just as I have obeyed my Father's commands and remain in his love" *(John 15:10)*.

What Christ wants from us is obedience to the Gospel, obedience to his commandments of love for God and love for our neighbour. At every moment of our lives, we must ask ourselves what Christ would want us to do in a particular situation; that is the only way to discover the truth, the only way to discover true freedom. Following Christ means giving freedom to the Father, being open to him, listening to him, and then we will receive true freedom from him. Our obedience is a radical surrender to God, that is the choice we have made, so that he may enter into our lives and lead us to true freedom. Following Christ means giving freedom to others, being open to them, listening to them, and then, in our turn, we will receive freedom from them. Our Lady set an example for us when she said, "I am the handmaid of the Lord; let what you have said be done unto me" *(Luke 1:38)*. Let us pray that we may be able to do the same in our lives; that we may listen to God's will for us, that we may be open to him, that we may choose to surrender in obedience to his commandments of love.

3rd Sunday of Easter

Acts 3: 13-15, 17-19   1 John 2: 1-5   Luke 24: 35-48

The understanding of the Old Testament in its fulfilment is an important stage in the discovery of the true meaning of Easter, for us as well as for the apostles. The People of God which is the Church is the inheritor of the promises made to Israel; this promise comes to its perfection in our lives of faith and service. It is an important theme in the stories of the risen Lord with his disciples, that he opened up the Scriptures to them.

FACING THE death and resurrection of Jesus Christ at Easter, we face our own death to sin and new life in Christ in Baptism. Because we live in a world of extended news bulletins, the crises across the nations which come into our homes and pressures of all kinds locally, it is difficult to stand back and make space for prayer. Yet this we must try to do if we are to escape from drowning in the ever encroaching waves of materialism. To stop, to make this space, is to battle against secular values. For many it may seem nonsense to resist and walk against the tide. But don't give up! Take courage! You will find spending time with God gives you a greater certainty and peace. Try a little each day. You will come to know yourself better and what to do for God and others.

I am sure part of us *really* believes in the power of prayer - and part of us is rather superficial and agnostic about God answering prayer. There is the story of an old lady who had a mountain behind her cottage. She read Christ's words 'if your faith is the size of a mustard seed you will say to this mountain 'move from here to there,' and it will move.' *(Matthew 17.20)* So one night she said in her night prayer, 'Lord, move this mountain' - and went to

bed. In the morning, she got up, looked out of the window, saw the mountain still there and said to God 'I knew you wouldn't move it!' Some expect too much in 'praying' for healing -some expect too little. Healing is in God's will and we must pray for healing deeply, intensely and yet not positively. It is God's gift - he loves us - trust him utterly and always say 'your will not mine be done'.

Finally - praying, healing, use of medicine - in everything we must remember each and all of us will die one day. Prepare for dying by living healthily, fully, prayerfully, and may God bless your efforts.

4th Sunday of Easter

Acts 4: 8-12   1 John 3: 1-2   John 10: 11-18

The Good Shepherd lays down his life and takes it up again. In this is the fulfilment of the mission that the Father gave Christ to complete and so in this he is glorified. Christ is, then, the unique source of salvation for everyone; hence, the early preaching of the apostles insists on this. For all those who believe in Christ, there is a destiny already mapped out - to be like God, to 'see him as he really is'.

WHAT WAS Jesus' vocation in life? Today's Gospel and all the Gospel passages help us to answer the question. How did Jesus know of his vocation, how did he come to know of his Father's will? Jesus was divine, he knew what his Father was to ask of him. I often ask what does the Father want me to do with the life he has given me. The answers are not always clear. I am confused. I have my doubts. Yes, I have anxieties. It was different for Jesus - or was it! I like the intimacy of Jesus and his Father. I like the times when I hear that Jesus goes alone to pray. I like that because I can identify myself with Jesus. I suppose that as Jesus journeyed through his life he too experienced difficulty.

Upon reflection, Jesus and I are not that separate in identifying our vocations and saying yes to the Father's will. I draw strength from knowing that I am a unique creation in God's hands. There will never exist anyone like me from the beginning of time to its end. So too I have a unique purpose in life. I may come to glimpse God's creative plan for me, or I may not. I am sure that I have purpose and that the Father will use me as his instrument.

Whether I see it or not, I do know that I must not allow myself to feel I am not worthy. I am worthy of God's calling. For some of us, we can see God's plan in our lives: a commitment in marriage; to lead a particular way of life in caring for the sick; teaching our children, or in service at God's table; in proclaiming the Word of God; as a religious sister, brother or priest. With reflection and prayer I discern God's call. In openness we offer our very selves. The opposite may be to say this is the honourable thing to do, when deep down within you know it is not right - to do so is to do violence to yourself. God wants what is good for you. In the Father's desire for us all, he wants us to be fully whole and holy, fully human, a creation of love that communicates God's love. It is our daily duty to talk and pray openly with our Father to sustain our calling: the very way in which Jesus found comfort in the Father's guidance.

5th Sunday of Easter

Acts 9: 26-31 1 John 3: 18-24 John 15: 1-8

The True Vine. Our life is bound up with that of Christ. To be his followers it is necessary for us 'to bear fruit', not just by 'words or mere talk'. The true test is whether we obey his commands or not; the response of the newly converted Paul is a model for our own. In the strength of the same Spirit which is given to us, we are to witness to the life of Christ within us.

ABOUT a hundred years ago, Sister Thérèse, who was then a Carmelite nun at Lisieux, wrote about her desires. She wanted to be a priest, a missionary, a martyr. Then she came across St. Paul's statement that there are faith, hope and love - but the greatest of these is love (*1 Corinthians 13:13*). At once she cried out in joy that she had finally found her vocation - to be love in the Church. St. Thérèse highlights for each of us - whatever other calling or vocation we may have - that the heart of any Christian

living must be love. This really is for each of us! But love is not just a nice word, a word to be used in song and on greeting cards or for young lovers. Earlier in the same chapter, St. Paul talks of love as patient, kind, does not take offence or store up grievances 'Love never comes to an end' (*1 Corinthians 13:5*) So we must realise and live out that everlasting love, because Jesus tells us to love one another as he loves us *(John 15:12*). This is a beautiful, joyful and fulfilling way of life. It is also a tough one to live, because it involves patience and suffering. Often we are not very good at giving ourselves in love. Bringing ourselves back to Christ's life, we have to realise that we are not given the example of just ideas or emotion in Jesus. At his own profound level *he gives himself in love*. Christ's love was and is for us and for all spirit and life.

6th Sunday of Easter

Acts 10: 25-26,34-5,44-8   1 John 4: 7-10   John 15: 9-17

The commandment of love. The love which God has shown us in Christ is above all else a practical love - it translates itself into action. Just as it broadens the scope of the Church, making it universal or 'catholic', it must enable us who profess to belong to that Church to reach out to everyone with the intensity of the love of Christ himself.

EVANGELISATION does not affect just one parish alone; it is something embarked on by the whole Church. Rather, then, than simply jumping in and thinking what we should do, we should look at what the Church has said on the subject. There are two main documents. They have the off-putting names of *Evangelii nuntiandi* and *Christifidelis laici*. They should be very much better known as the documents on Evangelisation and on the Laity. I wish, indeed, that they were better known. It saddens me when I hear Catholics say things like: "I never believe anything the Vatican says". Such comments are prejudiced and ignorant and, I suspect, are all too often based, not on a study of Vatican documents, but on superficial and biased newspaper comment.

Be that as it may, these two documents have particularly lovely things to say. As with all the

Vatican documents, they are not the easiest of reading, but by gosh, they are worth the effort. A particular model of the Christian life and of evangelisation emerges from them. It is rooted in prayer. Our starting point is our relationship with God and the way it is developed in prayer, through scripture, through the sacraments. As this relationship develops, so we change inside. As we change inside, so that changes the way we behave - not just in "Churchy" things, but in everything we do. Breathing the Spirit of Christ into all aspects of our lives is the way we build the kingdom of heaven. As our behaviour changes, so it is noticed by those who have not yet been set on fire by the Spirit. It is their interest in why we are as we are that opens them to being told the Good News of Christ. Evangelisation, therefore, can never be just a matter of shouting on street corners; it is a process that includes the whole of Christian witness.

Some people may already be fully committed to that model of the Christian life; they may need help in working out how they can breathe the Spirit of Christ into what they do at work or when they play sport or when they take political action. Others may be only just starting to develop their relationship with God; they may need help with different types of prayer. Yet others may have an active prayer life, but have not yet allowed that to change the way they behave; they may need to be shown activities into which they can be drawn. For those outside the Church, we need to find ways of making the faith ever more accessible to them. Two things we can be sure of: the Decade will call for a whole range of actions and not just one; and it certainly shouldn't be dull. If it is, we have only ourselves to blame!

The Ascension of the Lord

Acts 1:1-11 Ephesians 1:17-23 Mark 16:15-20

Though the Apostles stared after Jesus as he ascended to heaven they remember his words.to proclaim the Good News to all creation. They preached and the Lord worked with them. Through our own baptism we have been saved and have joined the body of Christ, the Church.

THE Ascension is an interesting feast. In life, you and I know how we come to say goodbye to someone who dies. It is a deeply moving experience in our lives: it leads to sorrow, guilt, bereavement. There is all the necessity and trauma of funeral arrangements, the service, the burial or cremation. We have experienced this. Our Lady and the disciples experienced it at the crucifixion. But now we have something very different.

You and I have lived through the post-resurrection accounts of Jesus and his appearances to his friends, but we are very different, because we know what happened afterwards. I think in meditating this week we would do well to imagine coming to the scene with the disciples and our foreknowledge. What is it all about? Is this really Jesus? We knew he was dead! Can he really be alive? Some still doubted, we are told. Jesus, knowing this, nevertheless gathered his friends round him and commissioned them- doubts included - to teach himself and his message to all the nations of the world.

Then he says goodbye! They are astonished all over again. This time Jesus doesn't die -he disappears! Are they now seeing things? Is this real? Open mouthed, they are suddenly told not to hang about goggle-eyed but to go and get on with the job of preaching the good news. But Jesus knew his friends! He knew his going was not enough. He told them to hold on before they went off preaching - to wait and to pray until the comforter, the paraclete, the promised Spirit came. This indeed they did and we wait with them today. So it is for us to enter into prayer, in faith and hope, as we join Our Lady and the Apostles in the first novena, the first nine days of prayer. I always love these nine days. It is an opportunity to have special prayers for the coming of the Holy Spirit. It is a beautiful way of preparing for the crowning feast of Pentecost.

7th Sunday of Easter

Acts 1: 15-17, 20-26   1 John 4: 11-16   John 17: 11-19

The mission of the Church. What has been received from God through Christ must be passed on through the life and work of the Church in all its members. Bound together in love, the Church is called upon to witness in every age to the God who reveals himself in Christ, so that God's love can be complete in us and in everyone who hears the Gospel.

THE DAYS between Ascension and Pentecost are the original days of prayer ordered by Jesus Christ himself before he left his followers to take back to his Father in heaven his total sacrifice made for us, to save us from sin and renew our relationship with God, the creator of life. He told his friends to wait for his sending of the Holy Spirit. In the life of the Church there are 'novenas'. These are sets of nine days dedicated to special prayers. Well, the original nine days were those between the Ascension and Pentecost. The passage in The Acts of the Apostles reads:

'Then they returned to Jerusalem from the hill called Olivet, which is near Jerusalem, no farther than a Sabbath day's journey. Entering the city they went to the room upstairs where they were lodging: Peter and John and James and Andrew, Philip and Thomas, Bartholomew and Matthew, James son of Alphaeus and Simon the Zealot, and Judas son of James. All these were constantly at prayer together, and with them a group of women, including Mary the mother of Jesus, and his brothers.'

(Acts 1:12-14) .

Let each of us, then, try to take a *little* more time to be peaceful, quiet and prayerful and let us *really* ask for the gift of the Holy Spirit next Sunday and into the future. We should be like the Apostles and Mary and shut out the world and let the Spirit come into our lives. We should look forward to being able to re-dedicate ourselves and being empowered with the gifts of the Spirit. Our prayer must be; Come, Holy Spirit, fill the hearts of the faithful.

Pentecost Sunday

Acts 2: 1-11   1 Corinthians 12: 3-7, 12-13   John 20: 19-23

The Spirit, the Gift of Christ. The dramatic manifestation of the coming of the Spirit on the Church enables us to see what he does - the apostles become fearless witnesses. And so all of us, no matter who we are, have this gift for our own salvation and the salvation of others. And so the Church goes on.

ONE OF the riches of the Spirit which is poured out on us is Joy - love, peace, joy, the list goes on. As Christians individually and as a group, we should be filled with joy. It should reflect from our hearts through our faces and our attitudes. It should be a source of joy picked up by others, reflected from one to another. If we helped others to be joyful would it not be a joy in itself for us? If people enjoyed meeting us, because of this radiation of the Spirit - if they found our company joyful and encouraging, helping them to live with more hope, trust, love and service of each other would that not be wonderful?

Jesus wanted his disciples to be filled with joy after the sorrows of the Passion and Cross. And indeed they were filled with joy when they saw him after the resurrection. But the fullness of that joy - and the other accompanying gifts and fruits of his coming were realised on the Day of Pentecost in the upper room - and then to all whom the apostles met afterwards.

More than this individual aspect, but partly springing from it, is the spirit of joy which should be in our worship. Do you think it does? I quite often find people who come to my Church as visitors telling me what a lovely, friendly feeling there is at Mass. Do you feel that in yours? It is part of what the Spirit of Joy should be, radiating from us as a congregation, a community, a people. Those who met the early Christian Church after Pentecost, used to feel this something. They used to say 'see how these Christians love one another.' Let us hope and pray in the celebration and follow up from the gift of the Spirit this Pentecost that we may grow in the Spirit and so help each other and those beyond our immediate fellowship to share love, joy, peace - the wonder of God's riches poured into our hearts.

Trinity Sunday

Deuteronomy 4:32-34,39-40 Romans 8:14-17 Matthew 28:16-20

Moses shows the people that there is only one Lord God and no other. Paul shows that the Spirit is active in the Church and lets us become children of God. Jesus shows that this happens through baptism.

TODAY IS Trinity Sunday. The Trinity is a problem for many Christians. Large numbers, I suppose, avoid thinking about it at all; others get very worried about not understanding something that is right at the centre of our faith. The various bits of the teaching are not difficult. We are able to think about the God who created heaven and earth, and about God coming to live as a man among us, and about the God we experience in our lives. In other words, we can cope with the ideas of God the Father, God the Son and God the Holy Spirit. Also, we can cope with the idea of there being one God only. Our problem comes if we try to put these ideas together.

So, does this mean that we should simply shrug our shoulders and put the Trinity on one side as something too complex for our poor minds. Not at all! We may not understand how it is that God can be both one God and also three persons, but we can draw great profit from meditating on the revelation that he is. For example, each of the three persons is complete and perfect in itself: Jesus is perfect as the Son, as a human being; the Spirit is perfect as the Spirit; the Father is perfect as the Father. Yet they are one God and that God is infinite and therefore cannot be divided. The three persons, therefore, must be bound together in the perfect unity of perfect love. We are called to become like God and so this is a model for us - and a very rich one. We are called, not only to become perfect persons, but also to be bound together in the perfect unity of perfect love. It is relatively easy to pursue one objective at the expense of the other. We have all met people who want to have unity at the cost of riding roughshod over the opinions and feelings of individuals; and today we meet an increasing number of people loudly shouting about their "right" to personal freedom irrespective of the values and consensus of the community in which they live - the community which alone makes their freedom possible. It takes very special people to be committed to both ideals at the same time; it takes people committed to growing in their understanding of God and committed to modelling their lives on that understanding; it takes people at whom the world marvels, saying "Lo! See how these Christians love one another".

8th Sunday of the Year

Hosea 2:16-17;21-22 2 Corinthians 3:1-6 Mark 2:18-22

In the midst of the desolation of the desert it is easier to find the Lord. Away from that which detracts us we ask if God will satisfy our hunger for him. The bridegroom, that is Jesus, has invited us to his wedding feast. In this feast, the Eucharist, we have our hunger satisfied until he comes again. This is the new covenant, that brings us to life, that Paul asks us to remember.

GOD'S LOVE for his creation is the theme which runs through all scripture. His relationship to us, his human creation, is one of love. His relation to his Church is one of love. And so in the length and breadth of the message many similes and parables are used of the lover, the bride, the bridegroom, the marriage feast and so on. The writers of Scripture were fond of using the 'heart' as an expression of the whole person. Though the mind was also used and hearing and understanding there was a deeper significance in the use of the *heart*.

In the second reading this Sunday, St. Paul (*2 Corinthians 3:1-6*) has a very beautiful rendering of this. He says he needs no letter of recommendation to or from the Corinthians because *they* are his letter 'written in your hearts that anyone can see and read.' It reminds me of the passage where others say 'see how these Christians love one another', which in turn makes me - and I hope us all - reflect on whether this can be said today of ourselves in our families and our local Church community?

Paul continues the metaphor:

> *It is plain you are a letter from Christ - written not with me but with the Spirit of the living God, not on some tablets, but on the tablets of your living hearts.*

Our hearts should be alive in God. We should always be open to hear his word and to let it speak to us when ever and where ever we are. When we do this we echo the disciples on the road to Emmaus after Christ's death who met him on the road and said to each other: 'Did not our hearts burn within us as he opened the Scriptures to us?' May this be the same in our lives as we think and pray over the Sunday liturgy.

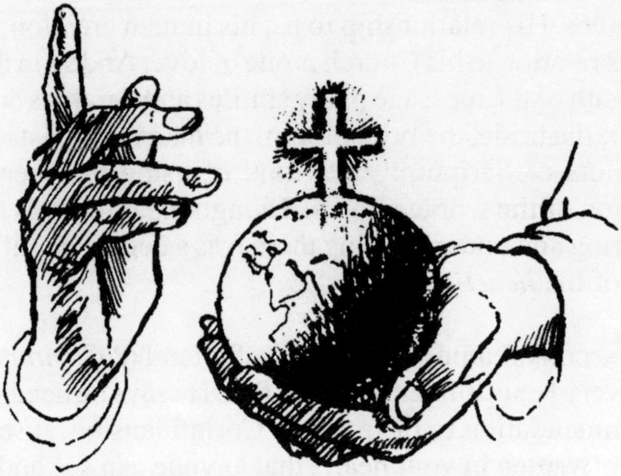

9th Sunday of the Year

Deuteronomy 5:12-15 2 Corinthians 4:6-11 Mark 2:23-3:6

The Sabbath was established for the good of all. It is a symbol of our freedom from the slavery of sin. Jesus likewise shows such freedom by showing mercy on the Sabbath. He shows that the guiding principles of love and charity should overcome the rules of our society. Paul reminds us that we are only 'earthenware jars' that draw our power from God.

THE BOOK of Genesis gives us a beautiful word-picture of God's creation of the world. It is fitted into the simple structure of six days, and then a lovely seventh day is added:

on the seventh day God had completed the work he had been doing. He rested on the seventh day after all the work had been doing. 'God blessed the seventh

> *day and made it holy, because on that day he rested after all his work of creating.*
>
> (*Genesis 2:2-3*).

Thus the pattern gives great emphasis to the seventh day, the Sabbath. The Jewish Faith, as in the Old Testament and Jesus' day, strictly maintains each Saturday as the Sabbath. Celebrating the Day of Resurrection and the Day of Pentecost, Christians changed the holy day to Sunday.

Those of us of some age remember a rather different feeling about Sunday from what is prevalent today. Personally, I am happy that the threat of damnation for deliberately not going to Mass on a Sunday is not the headline of teaching and preaching today. But, sadly, celebrating Mass individually, as families and as a community each Sunday, has suffered in recent years. This weekend the reading reminds us of Christ's teaching:

> *The Sabbath was made for man, not man for the Sabbath, so the Son of Man is master even of the Sabbath.*
>
> (*Mark 2:27-28*)

Mark may have written the first part of the sentence when the Jewish Sabbath was being marginalised by Christians. But today, it is men, women and children who emphasise that part, while very many ignore Jesus Christ as master of the Sabbath. It is vitally important for all of us to have some time off, to rest and relax, to be with family and friends. It is also vitally necessary to rest in the Lord, to worship and praise Jesus, Lord of the Sabbath. To welcome Him into ourselves, our homes and our families through the sacrament of his Body and Blood, which comes to us through the Eucharist. Let us all try our best to restore Sunday in our lives to God, allowing the seventh day of creation its proper, restful place at the centre of our being.

10th Sunday of the Year

Genesis 3:9-15   2 Corinthians 4:13 - 5:1   Mark 3:20-35

To accept the words and call of Christ is to be part of his family, indeed part of him. To reject them is to follow the path of the serpent (Satan). This is the path that leads to enmity between God and peoples and between peoples. Suffering, anguish and even death should not weaken our trust in the Lord. Jesus is stronger than evil and has promised us life to the full.

THERE IS so much loneliness about, in and among people today. This is particularly so in urban and inner city areas. Many go home from work to an empty bedsit or a small flat; many cannot even go out to work but simply live in one or two rooms. The latter may well be afraid to go out in the evening, if they go out at all, because of muggings and street violence. Some are simply shut in for reasons known only to themselves. Often, because a person is lonely, no one knows about the loneliness. It

is successfully hidden, making it all the more intense. The lonely person does not necessarily come out and shout about it, loneliness is endured, and built up behind closed, impersonal doors.

A Christian has a duty to try to help anyone in need. The lonely are people in need. How can a Christian help? It may mean keeping an eye and an ear open for them in the street, sharing your loneliness with them. It is possible and very useful to become able to pray with and for lonely people. They need help, so try to get to know how to be alongside them, how to ease their loneliness, how to be patient, listening, kind and constructive. The prayers which follow try to express some of this.

I'm very conscious, Lord, of all that you have given me
family, friends, a job, ability. Life is full and happy for me.
Thank you, Jesus, but I am also sure that some
I know are so shut in and lonely.
They seem to have no friends, no interest.
They get depressed and sad.
How can I help them, Lord?
Show me a way, because by myself I seem
useless and cannot get them out of themselves.

I pray for those who live alone and see no one who will talk to them;
those who encounter many people but are timid and cannot relate to any;
those who feel different and alien to the people they live among.

11th Sunday of the Year

Ezekiel 17:22-24   1 Corinthians 5:6-10   Mark 4:26-34

God has not abandoned us, He is still with us. Just as the small seed slowly grows to full maturity so does the word of God. Our life is already a sharing in the life of Christ but it has not yet achieved the full communion that God wants us to have. We should strive towards this communion and become a new shoot growing from our former selves.

GOD IS the first to know that it is not easy for human beings to take up the cross and follow Jesus Christ. That is why God sent his Son and commissioned him to preach and teach and above all give us the example of his life and death. In his life, Jesus prayed and worshipped giving us the lead. We must always strive to follow the example of Jesus and deepen our commitment to the Father. We should centre on our own personal life of prayer and on the Mass, the Eucharist. Here, at Mass, we meet Jesus in a very special way through his word in the readings and the homily and in Holy Communion. That is - if we come.

Prayer and the Eucharist are the foundation of our power to fulfil our commission of going out to teach the salvation gained for each and everyone by Jesus. To stay away from these wonderful gifts is to weaken ourselves, weaken the Church and weaken our witness in our homes and neighbourhood.

People often talk about the fact that more and more young people are leaving the Church . This is a great cause of sorrow in our lives. We must all realise that we have a part to play in bringing them to the Church. No, it is not easy to encourage children and young people to give time and interest to God and Church. But more is done by love and example than any other way. Take a short time thinking about yourself, God and the Gospel. Try always to share in the Mass, especially always receiving Holy Communion.

12th Sunday of the Year

Job 3:1,8-1   1 Corinthians 5:14-17   Mark 4:35-41

The sea was seen as the home evil powers, chaos and death. Only God could master the sea. By showing that he has power over the sea Jesus reveals that he is God. To accept this is to become a new creation, a new person in Christ. Not to do so is to be asked 'How is it you have no faith?'

BAPTISM AND Confirmation put us into the crowd of people that God has entrusted to give his GOOD NEWS to others. It is important to say that! You and I are ENTRUSTED by God. He must have a lot of trust, mustn't he? God expects each of us to come to know the content of his Good News. If we are going to be effective from his point of view, it is our individual responsibility to know our Faith. This is no easy task, is it? Just to get the bare bones, as it were, must take our time, our interest and our perseverance. What is more, we need to work and pray for a continual growth. What we learn at home or at school as children and young people is not enough for life. It should be reinforced and developed as our years and our experience develop.

A lot of people feel inadequate when it comes to talking about their belief. Well - that is quite natural - even for the greatest theologian there should be the awe and humility of trying to grapple with and explain the mysteries of God. Does that let people off the hook? Can they leave it just to these learned people? The answer is no. Often the deep things of God are 'revealed to mere children'. You and I need to trust God as God trusts us and, while striving to learn more of him through prayer, reading and discussion, to rely also on his Spirit to enlighten us and put the right words on our lips.

13th Sunday of the Year

Wisdom 1:13-15;2:23-24 2 Corinthians 8:7,9,13-15 Mark 5:21-43

Jesus is a healer, but he is also more than that. He gives salvation and eternal life to all who recognise him as their Lord. He shares with us all the riches of his life. Paul reminds us that we too should share with those who are poorer than us. In healing Jairus's daughter and the sick woman Jesus shows that salvation is upon them all.

IF WE accept, as we should do, the call by Jesus Christ to each and everyone of us to take up the cross and follow him, what does this mean to us? Following Christ is for each of us both individually and together. Individually, each of us is responsible for our own development. In our personal life, there is no substitute for growth in our relationship with Jesus. If we want to be close to him, we must give him time in prayer. Normally, this should be time given once or twice every day for some minutes or longer. To this we should add glances at God as we move about during the day - in short prayers praising, thanking and asking him. We can also join a prayer group or form one ourselves.

Mass is our central prayer. Here we come together to pray and to worship. It is so important that we **do** come to worship at Mass together, that our Church long ago put us under obligation to go each week regularly, if we possibly can. When we fall away from Mass-going we can easily fall from ordinary personal prayer as well. Now, it is not only through prayer that we follow Christ. He also asks us to love our neighbour. This we can do partly by praying for our neighbour. But Jesus expressed his love in service as well. He went about healing and doing good. He gave the example of washing the feet of his disciples.

We add to the life we have in prayer the great command of love. To pray is only half the story. We must put our Christian commitment into action. To reach out and become a 'slave of the needs of others' is to do what Christ did.

14th Sunday of the Year

Ezekiel 2:2-5 1 Corinthians 12:7-10 Mark 6:1-6

The speakers of truth, the prophets know that they may well come up against opposition. But they have been called and must speak the Lord's words. Jesus received hostility from his own people who, through their lack of faith, did not recognise him as their saviour. Like Paul we should recognise the fact of Christ working through us and how much we have received from Him.

AMOS WAS a shepherd and looked after sycamores; Peter and Andrew and James and John were simple fishermen. They were not highly educated, they were not great scholars, they were not trained priests or rabbis, yet God called each of them to go out and preach his word. We all of us know that we are called to spread the good news of Christ - and most of us find it difficult to do. We do not think we know enough to preach it properly - neither did

Amos. We do not feel worthy - well, we're not, no-one is, but God calls us nevertheless. We feel embarrassed if we seem to be preaching to others, if we seem to be setting ourselves up as holier than them - we are right to feel embarrassed if that's what we're doing, but that's not spreading God's word.

Many people have quite the wrong idea of what the word is about. It is not me saying to someone else: "I've got all the answers, so you've got to believe what I believe and do what I say". As Christians we believe in God and our strongest desire is to get closer to him. If we do not have that belief or that desire, we have no basis for being Christians. We also know that we actually get closer to God by imitating the life and example of Jesus and by participating in the Church he gave us.

I think of the Church as being like one of those wagon trains we used to see on cowboy movies. Each wagon has its own family and identity and each has its own character and skills, yet they are all going in the same direction and whenever there is a problem everyone rallies round to share their skills and expertise and give the help needed. Because the train has a common purpose its members accept a degree of authority from the leader about the direction to go and the route to follow, but this authority does not prevent the personal growth and development of the people in the train. When we think of the Church in this way, we can see that spreading the word is really about sharing the insights and understandings that we have. In each person's journey towards God, there is the need to take Jesus' teaching and example and apply it to the special circumstances of the person's life. Just like the people on the wagon train, we pool our resources and try to help each other on this journey - and it is the height of arrogance to think that we do not need such help. The teaching of the Church is really nothing more than the accumulation of all these insights and sharings by all sorts of people over twenty centuries. Some teaching is very clear-cut, some is much more tentative - but all of it is intended to help us make our own journeys.

15th Sunday of the Year

Amos 7:12-15   Ephesians 1:3-14   Mark 6:7-13

Like the disciples we must spread the message of the Son of God to all we meet. We should not be ashamed of who we are and should not soften the message we hold to be true. Like Amos we should obey God and not those around us. The message that we hold dear is that Jesus is the Christ who has brought the Kingdom of God to the world and invites all to choose to be part of it.

IN THE ceremony of Baptism, the parents of the child to be baptised are asked to accept responsibility to bring the child up in the knowledge of God and his commandments. They say they are willing. Later the priest says they are to be the first and best of teachers.

It is interesting that frequently in talking with mothers and fathers, some are inclined to say that *they* cannot teach their children - 'That is for you to do, Father, or the nuns or the Catholic School. We don't know enough.' Now that is sad because it is probably not true. It is their diffidence, perhaps encouraged by priest and teachers, implying our superiority. But it can also reflect on their parents and teachers who do not seem to have given them the confidence to help their young people.

Some of the prophets felt the same reluctance when God tells them to prophesy. For instance in today's First Reading (*Amos 7:12-15*) Amos says:

> *I was no prophet, neither did I belong to any of the brotherhoods of prophets. I was a shepherd and looked after sycamores, but it was the Lord who took me from herding the flock and said to me 'Go, prophesy to my people Israel.*

Many parts of the faith and of scripture we do not understand ourselves. Always we must hope to grow - a whole lifetime of growth and at the end, may we grow into Christ in eternal life.

I confess I often feel like that when someone asks me a question. I have no idea how to put an answer which will mean anything. I try a quick prayer - often I am still at a loss and so do not be surprised if you are too. But don't just give up. It is not infrequent that if you have the patience to listen and let the other person talk they almost work out their own difficulty and feel you have helped them. For ourselves - perhaps we can suggest they come again, can ask a friend for help.

16th Sunday of the Year

Jeremiah 23:1-6 Ephesians 2:13-18 Mark 6:30-34

Jesus is the true shepherd of his flock, foretold by Jeremiah, who is moved to pity for his people. He will gather all peoples to himself and bring reconciliation to a divided world. He is not like the false shepherds of Israel who scatter the people of God. By the shedding of his blood he has shown himself to be the true king exhibiting love, honesty and integrity.

THOSE PEOPLE who have come to my room over the years will have seen hanging from the lamp on my desk a sign which reads 'BLESS THIS MESS'. (I sometimes say God has heard my prayer and blesses it - and it has increased and multiplied!) I wonder whether your life is very ordered or a 'mess'. It is worth thinking about, because it is often true that because we are so arranged, essential things get pushed aside - we don't have time. It may be time for God and prayer (very common, I'm afraid).

It may be for spending enough time with husband, wife, children, friends; for fixing something in the flat or room; for visiting someone in hospital, for sitting back and sorting yourself out, for writing that letter.

On the other hand, some people are so tidy, they shut out the possibility of breaking routine and so become rigid and inflexible, building a wall round their treasured routine - nothing must be changed. This means any change in personal life, society or the Church is rejected. But change aids growth. Our lives without being just a mess need a mixture of stability and change. New ideas and new ways of thinking and living and loving develop us. If we keep them and ourselves open before God in prayer, we can recognise God in the daily happenings which mould and change our lives. So do not be afraid! You and I are in God's hands and even the most unexpected and unpleasant happenings have a part to play. These are, too, the wonderful changes. As I often say to others - make time to love yourself a bit.

17th Sunday of the Year

2 Kings 4:42-44 Ephesians 4:1-6 John 6:1-15

Jesus has taken an act like that of Elisha and added a new meaning. In feeding the five thousand he gives freely in such abundance that all comers were satisfied with plenty left over. In the Eucharist he has given us food for our journey in which our needs are satisfied. However Paul reminds us that this gift demands that we act and be unity in the one body.

YOU CANNOT privatise the Mass. The Mass is offered for everyone. That is what the bidding prayers are about. All the Eucharistic Prayers make clear the range of people the Mass is offered for. One of the reasons that I love the fourth Eucharistic Prayer is that is does not leave out anyone:

> *Lord, remember those for whom we offer this sacrifice, especially N. our Pope, N. our bishop, and bishops and clergy everywhere. Remember those who take part in this offering, those here present and all your people, and all who seek you with a sincere heart. Remember those who have died in the peace of Christ and all the dead whose faith is known to you alone.*

It is wonderful; it is not limited to Catholics, it is not limited to Christians, it is all-embracing. The Mass is the sacrifice of Christ - who came for the salvation of the whole world. What are we doing when we ask for a Mass intention? Well, we are asking the priest to include that intention in his prayers during the Mass. It is not something that involves the rest of the congregation. Indeed, if there are other priests concelebrating the Mass, each of them may well have a separate and different intention. Over the centuries the asking for Mass intentions has won an important place in the hearts of many people - and that can be nothing but good. It is a source of great consolation to people bereaved to know that their loved one is being thought about and prayed for. It can provide a focus for concentrating our prayers in a special way when we are facing a particular problem or challenge. But it is not something to be used lightly or frivolously; it is not a piece of magic.

It is praying and offering sacrifice for a person in the most intimate way possible. In the mass we remind the Father what his Son Jesus has done for us. We remind the Father that his Son's death means that we have been redeemed and have been given a place in his Kingdom. To couple this with a prayer for a particular person is to offer that memorial to the Father for that person. What more wonderful gift is there that we can give to anyone?

18th Sunday of the Year

Exodus 16:2-4,12-15 Ephesians 4:17,20-24 John 6:24-35

Jesus tells those who have come to follow him because of the feeding of the five thousand that he is the living bread which comes down from heaven. Just as the Israelites received the manna as a sign of God's love for them we have the Eucharist as a sign of the love of Jesus on the cross. By sharing in this gift we are called to become more like Christ and live in God's way.

THERE IS no doubt that the human race is good at complaining not least the people of Israel, not least ourselves. And so we begin today with the Jews complaining to Moses in the desert and God's forgiveness and bounty provides 'bread from heaven', manna in the desert. What a wonderful response to their complaining - and it is of course our direct link through to Christ, the bread of life. For Jesus after feeding the multitude left them and they went after him and he scolded them saying they only came because they had been fed. And then he tells them it was not Moses but his Father in heaven who gave them bread in the desert.

It might be thought that by this time in history, the human race would have achieved a greater level of overall standard of living. On the one hand there have been almost incredible developments in science and technology. Even though there have been some significant new improvements in basic crops there are still vast areas of malnutrition, crop failure, life on the breadline and actual starvation and famine.

Throughout history, needless to say, food has been centrally important to the people of God's creation and so it is realistic to find our scriptures woven through with plenty of stories that deal with food failure, relating to food and so on. Eventually the reader of the Bible comes to the main celebration left to us by Jesus - his supper, his bread and wine, his body and blood in the Eucharist.

This is the first of a series of extracts which cover the next two or three Sundays on Jesus' theme of the bread of life. It gives us the chance to ponder various aspects of the theme which, hopefully, will enrich our understanding of the Eucharist.

19th Sunday of the Year

1 Kings 19:4-8 Ephesians 4:30 - 5:2 John 6:41-51

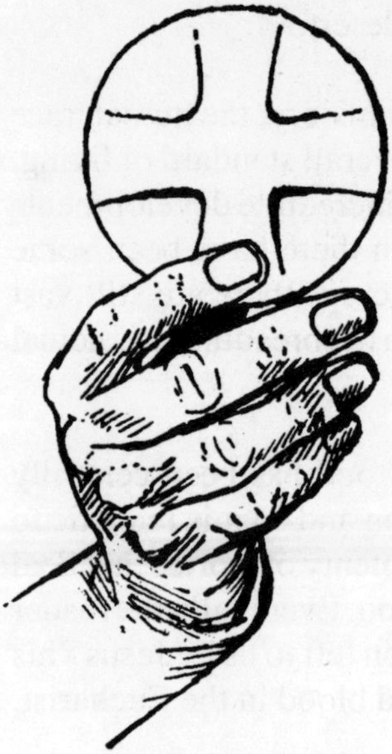

We are on a journey to God, which lasts a lifetime not forty days. We journey under the love and protection of the Trinity. Under the guidance of the Holy Spirit we aim to be more like the Father by loving Him as Christ did. Like Elijah our journey is sustained by the bread. As it is only through Christ and him alone can we come to the Father.

CONTINUING the theme of the bread of life, we have the story of Elijah (*1 Kings 19:17-81*) when he is in very real despair and falls asleep as we can often do when tired out with troubles. But he was awoken and told to eat the heavenly food provided. He eats, sleeps and is again told when to eat and go on his way - which he does for forty days and nights to God's mountain, Horeb. We are not ourselves able to live on bread from heaven alone, but we should not underestimate its power in us when we receive Holy Communion.

The Gospel finds the Jews complaining again - this time because they say they know Jesus is son of Joseph yet he is claiming 'I am the bread that came down from heaven.' Jesus tells them off and declares his closeness to his Father who sent him, reiterates the passing value of humanity in contrast to himself, the living bread come down from heaven - his flesh for the life of the world.

When the Eucharist is celebrated by the Church, the celebrant after the consecration, asks us to 'proclaim the mystery of faith'. Each time we share at Mass we are confronted by this mystery of faith. Because we are human, we may be distracted or bored and find we utter the proclamation unthinkingly or like robots. There is a sense in which the Mass is all too quick and even receiving Holy Communion can be over in a flash. It is difficult to know what can be done. Some sing a hymn, some have a varied length of silence after communion. Some parishes cut the number of masses celebrated and give more time and space for each celebration. It would be a good idea to take a personal or a group look at your local situation and see if you can formulate possible ways forward. It is probably true that there are varied opinions, some really wanting a quick-in-quick-out mass to do little more than fulfil the obligation. Others would want more. Think about it.

It would help if people think about what they want from the mass. Do they want to get it over and done with? They may think that they would want it to finish so that they can get on with the rest of their lives. Do people want to pause a bit and take stock? They may see the mass as an oasis in the rest of their otherwise busy lives. Do people want to praise the Lord in song and gesture? They may think the mass to be a time when they are most free to be themselves. Or people want a mixture of these, wanting one type rather than another a different times? I think that we should indeed have Catholic tastes, we should be open to all types of liturgy and see that what may not help us may indeed be helpful to others. After all there is only one Lord and one Spirit which we all share.

20th Sunday of the Year

Proverbs 9:1-6   Ephesians 5:15-20   John 6:51-58

Jesus, the risen one, is in communion with us for all time through his body and blood. To share in both is to be part of him. To eat the bread and drink the wine that has been prepared for us is to leave behind our folly and draw life from Christ. To do so is to redeem the world by the example of the life we lead.

THE VERY word 'Eucharist' means thanksgiving, which is another way for us to continue on the theme of these weeks - the bread of life come down from heaven.

As a generalisation, I wonder what you would think of a proposition that we are a pretty ungrateful lot? If you look around at yourself and at others, do you get the sense that, like the Jews, we are better at complaining and finding fault than being grateful? It is rather like the picture of a person to whom you say 'Isn't it a lovely day' and the response is 'Yes, but it's going to rain this evening !'

St. Paul, writing to the Ephesians in this Sunday's second reading (*Ephesians 5:15-20*)

> *Sing the words and tunes of the psalms and hymns when you are together and go on singing and chanting to the Lord in your hearts, so that always and everywhere you are giving thanks to God.*

That is a good idea and though it is impractical to be singing psalms all the time, it should certainly encourage us to make the Eucharist we share a really happy, joyful occasion. When we are glad to be there we want to share with others, we are happy to sit

next to someone and not hide behind a pillar, we enjoy sharing the peace with others.

The thanksgiving sharing of the Eucharist should make us want to go from it into the rest of our lives hoping others will pick up the sense of joy and thanksgiving from us. One of the practices I like to share, which is not specifically Eucharistic, is that when I wake up in the morning, the first thing I do is to make the sign of the cross and say 'Thank you, God' - for yesterday, for the night, for the day which is coming - Thank you God. Why not try something like that?

21st Sunday of the Year

Joshua 24:1-2,15-18   Ephesians 5:21-32   John 6:60-69

Like the disciples and the tribes of Israel we have a choice, to follow the will of God or not. Do we give ourselves freely and without reservation to being followers of Christ, just as husband and wife become one? For the faithful ones there can be no answer other than that of Peter "we believe"

THE EUCHARIST is the Sacrament of Unity, yet it has also been a great source of division. Anyone who has been at all involved in a liturgy group, a choir, the arrangement of flowers even will understand what I mean when I say how divisive the preparation of the liturgy can be. Perhaps it is that everything connected is so close to our hearts we are particularly possessive and edgy.

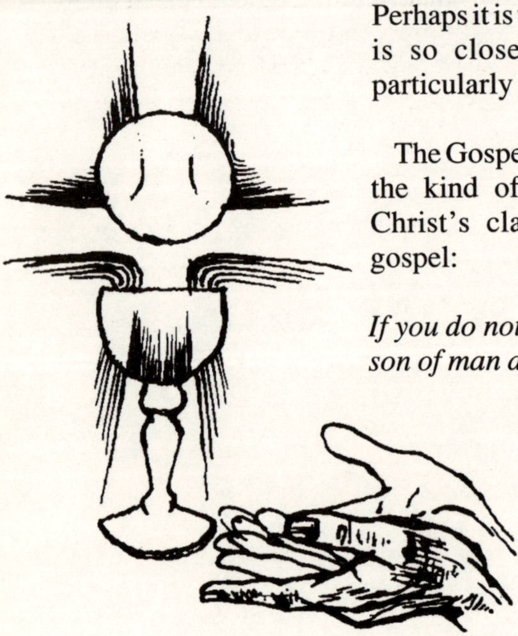

The Gospel story gives us a lead into the kind of situation which arises. Christ's claim from last Sunday's gospel:

If you do not eat the flesh of the son of man and drink his blood, you will not have life in you

This is too much and the followers of Jesus exclaim:

This is intolerable language. How could anyone accept it? And many of the disciples left him and stopped going with him.

Over the centuries, there have been very many tensions, theological disputes and even the break up of the Church, not least at the time of the Reformation when the issue of transubstantiation became a central point of theological/philosophical debate. It remains today a main stumbling block - the question of inter-communion being very touchy.

The Catholic Church has also suffered much from the rigours of Jansenism, with its view that the things of the body are evil, which made the worthiness to receive Holy Communion a real mountain to climb. More recently, with the loss of the Tridentine Rite, Vatican II changes in the liturgy and with receiving Holy Communion in the hand, many like the disciples of the Gospel have turned away. Why is this? What has made so many people so disillusioned that they leave the Church? Could it be that there is a sense of possessiveness in people's attitude to the Eucharist? So much so that when the way that they wish to receive it is changed they turn away? Perhaps they feel lost, hurt or even betrayed. Yes - the Eucharist still is sadly divisive.

22nd Sunday of the Year

Deuteronomy 4:1,2,6-8 James 1:17-18,21-22,27 Mark 7:1-8,14-15,21-23

Jesus wants us to love the Lord with all of our being. He has no time for the type of hypocrisy that thinks that as long as you act in such and such a way it does not matter what is in your heart. He shows the Scribes and Pharisees that all the rules that they have added to the Law of Moses do not change the heart. God's call to holiness demands a change of heart which is shown by the love we share and our integrity.

MOSES AND the Law are once more put before us and linked with Jesus Christ's teaching. The first reading (*Deuteronomy 4*) shows Moses laying out the law as a way and guideline to be observed carefully so that the people of Israel may enter the land promised by the Lord. They will also be seen as wise and understanding by others. Moses, though he gave the law firmly, saw the acceptance and keeping of it as something to give Israel the status and respect of a great nation, asserting no other nation was so close to God or had laws and customs to match this whole Law. As we know if we read these earlier books, there were very detailed and numerous injunctions set down and these became more and more oppressive and binding under the guidance of the Scribes and Pharisees.

And so Christ, in his own day, hit out at the Scribes and Pharisees for placing impossible burdens on people. Today's reading (*Mark 7*) finds Jesus up against just this kind of situation where he is attacked because his disciples do not do the custoMary washing of hands and arms before they eat. Jesus refers them to Isaiah who he says speaks of them when he writes:

> *This people honours me only with lip-service, while their hearts are far from me.*

For ourselves, we are once more asked to look at our own lives. Are we just paying lip-service to the teachings of Christ and his Church? Is our worship worthless? Are the doctrines we teach and use 'only human regulations'? Worship, prayer, way of life - each must have not just the letter of the law which kills but the Spirit of the Law which makes us live. That Spirit of the law can be summed up in the one great command to *love*. God and Neighbour, both must be the foci of our love.

23rd Sunday of the Year

Isaiah 35:4-7 James 2:1-5 Mark 7:31-37

James tells us that there should not be a class distinction in our faith, the two are not compatible. As Isaiah foretold Jesus, the Messiah, made the ears of the deaf unsealed and the tongue of the dumb sing. Here he shows his lack of discrimination by healing someone from a pagan area. This still challenges us today. Do we show discrimination?

ONCE MORE this weekend, we are pointed by the Scripture readings to the caring centre of the teaching in both Old and New Testaments. Specifically, Isaiah is encouraging those of faint heart. As I understand, it certainly refers to me and to each and everyone. However brave or hard or self-confident anyone is, we all need support and caring from others - and hopefully one or two with whom we grow close. Caring and sharing is not easy. In particularly, it is not easy all the time, day in and day out (when everything goes wrong, there is no human response, and God, if he is there at all, seems unloving and unjust). I think this kind of depression hits us all at times and for some it is much longer lasting. Jesus came especially for the poor - and in this he came for all. We need the humility to accept that we are all rich before God, because we are all poor before God. This paradox is clear because all we have and are is from God's gift of life and love. What a rich gift is life, even when it seems to us to be blighted by some disability.

Christ himself did some physical healing - the deaf, the dumb and blind. But in real terms this was only the tip of the iceberg, Christ's main purpose went deeper than the physical. Each of us is blind, deaf, dumb and lame in our seeing, hearing, speaking and spreading the Good News Jesus brings. This is where we all need courage - need not to be afraid. It is easy for me to write that it is a fearful thing to fall into the hands of the living God. It is easy to write that this costs not less then everything. To live this is not easy. 'Do not be afraid', says the song, 'for I am with you'. So what I am trying to say is that we are all afraid to accept that we are afraid. We must face this fear. The fear can be to believe - or to open our eyes to our own needs and others - or to get involved, to commit ourselves. We fear to let go in prayer. Often we fear to come out and share our Catholic faith - be not afraid! You have a lot to give. You do not have to go through a course. But we can help you if you need ideas. You are on the ground, near your neighbour.

24th Sunday of the Year

Isaiah 50:5-9 James 2:14-18 Mark 8:27-35

Peter is right when he calls Jesus the Christ. Jesus shows that when we accept this we are called to act. To take up our cross, stand up to the world for the Lord is our vindicator. A faith that does not act in the world is not in full communion with Christ. In following the example of the disciples and Christ we show our faith is fully alive.

ONE OF the main issues of the Reformation, was the discussion and disagreement about the theology of justification by faith alone. St. James (*James 2:14-18*) in our second reading today cites the case of 'someone who has never done a single good act but claims he has faith. Will that faith save him?' and after citing another instance of uselessness by refusing to help someone in need, he goes on: 'Faith is like that - if good works do not go with it, it is dead.' He is really doing no more than underlining what Jesus says elsewhere 'By their fruits you will know them.' For he tells his listeners to say to such people

I will prove to you that I have faith by showing you my good deeds - now prove to me you have faith without any deeds to show.

Today there is much less emphasis on justification by faith alone and the pendulum has swung the other way, so that if anything, people are relying too heavily on *doing* and not enough on *faith*, or on *being*. To be over busy may diminish reliance upon God in faith and the concentrated effort of endeavouring to do everything by oneself without reference to God. There is indeed much to be done in almost every direction. There never seems enough time or enough people to work. But the balance is enormously important and there is no way that St. James would want us to do the good deeds without faith. It is also particularly necessary to realise at the end of each day that not all has been achieved and much we must leave to God, as we go to bed saying our prayers.

Without giving time to the Lord we run the very real risk of 'burnout' in what we do. The situation has happened again and again; people feel that they can get on with their lives without the Lord. All they need is themselves. Even if they are committed in their faith they feel that they are too busy to pray to the Lord and deepen their relationship with him. When things start to go wrong then they have no-one to turn to. They have not had the practice of immersing themselves in the Lord and are lost. Do not become like them.

25th Sunday of the Year

Wisdom 2:12, 17-20 James 3:16 - 4:3 Mark 9:30-37

There is division in the world. People want to be greater than each other and through jealousy lay traps for the virtuous. Even the disciples wondered who was the greatest among them. All this is because the human heart is divided. Only when we let ourselves to be taught by God, as a little child would, do we become pure of heart.

CHRISTIANITY is a web of paradoxes and often seeing contradictions. The example given us this week is from the whole Gospel passage (*Mark 9:30-37*). Jesus comes for everyone, but God's plan does not overwhelm us as he could do. The whole world could have a Damascus Road conversion like Paul but that is not God's way because he treats us, knows us and loves us as individuals. Even in the short span he lived on earth he took his time. Choosing those he wanted close to him, he took his time before revealing everything to them. In today's Gospel, he avoids others because he does not want people to know he is instructing his disciples.

Indeed what he was teaching they did not understand because it was about his being put to death and then rising - what extraordinary teaching ! Their basic thought was like the world's thought. We spend our time trying to get on to have better jobs, better pay, better homes - up and up. And Jesus is saying to them 'If anyone wants to be first, he must make himself last of all and servant of all.' Here is the paradox. It is difficult to see in the disciples' day how these simple men could grasp the point. Surely this remains true today in the frightening competition of education, job-seeking and career climbing.

But the disciples at this stage had been in the process of jockeying for position - a situation which occurs on a number of occasions in the Gospel story. Jesus continues with the illustration of the little child, setting this child as their model. What a difficult concept - simplicity, directness, acceptance of these, and so often a child has a depth of insight beyond anything we older people achieve.

In our day, St. Thérèse of Lisieux gives her interpretation of spiritual childhood. Her 'little way' deserves to draw many followers. Because it give an attainable path to holiness.

26th Sunday of the Year

Numbers 11:25-29   James 5:1-6   Mark 9:38-43, 45, 47-48

The Spirit of the Lord is offered to all. There is no inner circle of faith that the Spirit is confined to. The elders in the desert and the man working in the name of Christ show they have the Spirit in them. If only we all did! That was the prayer of Moses and is the wish of Christ. If we did, there would be no injustice in the world and no more sin.

THE TEACHING of the Catholic Church has always been that she is the one true Church. This has been a very strong doctrine leading to the statement 'no salvation outside the Church'. Now there have been many variations and in more, especially post

Vatican II years, a broadening approach to other Christian Churches and denominations and also to other faiths. The whole ecumenical movement has grown and developed, there is much more openness, but in many ways there are wide gaps of difference and no inter-communion.

Having said this, it is interesting to have two readings looking at prophesying and healing being worked by 'outsiders'. In the first, we have Moses' spirit being shared out by God on seventy elders, so that they prophesied. But two stayed in camp and the spirit fell on them also, which caused consternation in the camp. A young man ran to tell Moses and Joshua wanted to stop them but Moses' reaction was 'the whole people of the Lord were prophets and the Lord gave the Spirit to them all.' How can this be? Surely there is a hierarchy in the Church! But this shows that the Spirit is for all.

Jesus had a similar experience when John complained that they had seen a man who was not one of them casting out devils in Jesus' name. John wanted him to be stopped. Jesus' reaction was not to stop him, saying that anyone working a miracle in his name is not likely to speak evil of him. 'Anyone who isn't against us is for us.'

This is a very broad statement and more and more people, groups and sects are springing up to preach and lead in Christ's name. We have quite a task to be discerning in this climate so that we do not condemn any non-Catholic or even Catholic we do not approve of. May the Spirit guide us and them.

27th Sunday of the Year

Genesis 2:18-24 Hebrews 2:9-11 Mark 10:2-16

Man and woman are made by God, therefore their coming together is not to be taken lightly, but as part of God's will. It is not something that should be considered as part of the law but something that God has a part in. A sign so wonderful it is used to describe the relationship of Christ to the Church.

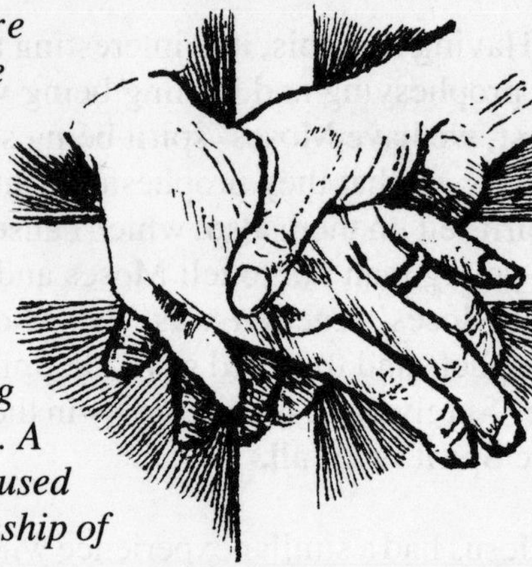

GOD IN the creation story this Sunday says "It is not good that man should be alone." *(Genesis 2:18)* He is talking of the two sexes supporting each other in their existence. In some situations in life it is good for us, women and men, to be alone with God. The difficulty of modern living is that conditions cramp us together in the inner city, in closely built homes, on the crowded streets, in buses or on the underground. Family life is crowded and rushed with much coming and going, both parents working, children at school, or a one parent condition. Only a few privileged 'ordinary people' have the time or freedom to go away to be alone with God. If you are so privileged try to go! But what of those many, many who are unable 'to escape' or even do not see 'escaping' as any part of their life, and even think it wrong to abandon the family for a selfish aloneness with God. Both spiritually and psychologically it is *extremely fruitful* (and recognised as such by Christian psychologists and un-religious psychologists alike) to put into your day a regular time for withdrawal. Many people now do half an hour of meditation each morning and evening. If you cannot do that - could you be alone at some time each day and give it to God? Try something regularly - however small.

Finally there are those who are not deprived of aloneness, but forced into it. You live alone in a flat, maybe housebound or bereaved or shy of company. In your situation - do all you can to create this space into something lovely, to be shared with Jesus. You are not alone because Jesus is there with you - it may not be easy to 'realise' he is with you. If you can do so, this gives you a sense of companionship and care. Please also invite the parish community to visit you, pray with you, give you Holy Communion, have a cup of tea. So crowded, make space! Alone - welcome Jesus and stay with him, and welcome in the community. We must all learn to be together and alone. Difficult, but possible, especially with the Spirit in us and God with us.

28th Sunday of the Year

Wisdom 7:7-11 Hebrews 4:12-13 Mark 10:17-30

Jesus, in love shows the rich man how to be a follower of his. To lose everything was too much for the man, that should not be the case with us. We must have the courage to follow the way of the Lord wholeheartedly. The Word of the Lord cuts through all our trappings of wealth and speaks to the heart. It is a call to put everything second to the love he has given us.

I THINK one of the stories in the Gospel which I get most out of is told in today's gospel reading (*Mark 10:17-30*). It is the story of the rich young man who dashes up to Jesus and asks 'What must I do to inherit eternal life?' Jesus replies by reciting to him the commandments. The young man says he has kept all these from his earliest days. Then Jesus says he lacks one thing

Go and sell everything you own and give the money to the poor - then come and follow me.

This was too much for the young man and he went away, sad.

Several things speak to me and I hope this may speak to you as well. I like the brashness of the young man in stating he had kept all the commandments from his earliest days! I could not do that - could you? Then there is a lovely touch in Mark 'Jesus looked steadily at him and loved him!' Don't you think that is wonderful? Jesus saw him as he was. He may have sensed that his next words about giving away all his possessions would be too much to ask - but he still loved him. What confidence this gives that Jesus really does see us as we are. He knows our imperfections and our weaknesses - and he still loves us! Ponder that in reference to yourself.

And the other thing which I find consoling is that the young man may later on have been able to face giving up all he possessed and he may have followed Christ. I have certainly found in listening to people that something which is impossible today may after weeks, months and even years become possible in a person's life. I have such confidence in God's love and care for individuals. If we are patient and work forward, praying and listening to Christ in our lives, we can have great hope in the Lord's gentle, loving lead.

29th Sunday of the Year

Isaiah 53:10-11   Hebrews 4:14-16   Mark 10:35-45

Jesus, our high priest, perfect and eternal has shown us the way. He understands the suffering and trials of our life. He has suffered in his service to his Father. If we do the same what praise would we expect? Our only ambition should be to serve the Father as Christ did. To pass through our trials to the Father as Christ did.

APART FROM the time when we celebrate the passion and death of Christ at the end of Lent and the daily reminder of the sacrifice of the Mass, fairly frequently in the prophets and in the New Testament we come across the suffering of Jesus Christ.

Isaiah's well-known passage which is our first reading today (*Isaiah 53:10-11*) is his prophecy of the suffering servant. He states quite clearly the offering of his life in atonement, then when his anguish is over 'he shall see the light and be content.' The picture spreads over far more than these few verses and is one of mockery, derision, abuse and degradation which make him unrecognisable, a worm and no man. Reading these passages especially at any time when one doubts God's love or the cost he has been prepared to pay, I find very salutary. It sets me back, takes me away from self-pity and brings a sense of proportion and reality to the little I suffer or endure compared to the wounds and agonising death of Jesus Christ for me - for us. 'By his suffering shall my servant justify many, taking their faults on himself.'

Over *against* this sombre *and* heart-rending picture, the Gospel tells us of the sons of Zebedee who are asking Jesus to put them on his right and left in his Kingdom. Jesus says it is not for him to promise - but can they drink the cup of suffering he has to drink?

Boldly they say they can. I wonder if they really understood what they were saying yes to. So Jesus says this baptism will happen and ends with repeating their need not to become great and first but a servant.

> *For the Son of Man did not come to be served, but to serve, to give his life for a ransom for many.*

How often we need to be reminded of this!

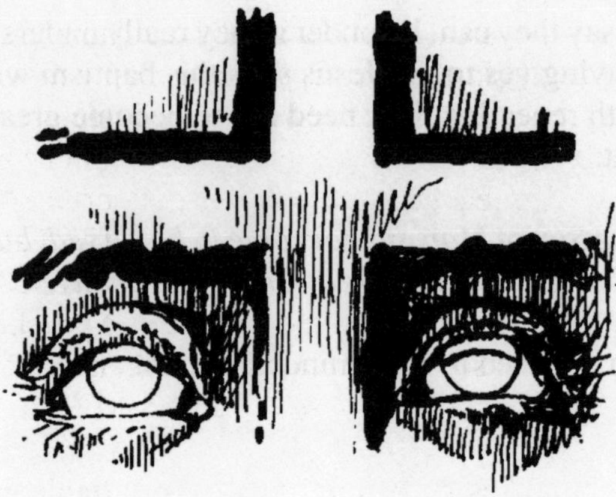

30th Sunday of the Year

Jeremiah 31:7-9 Hebrews 5:1-6 Mark 10:46-52

Jesus gives sight to a blind man who with a clear insight of faith recognises him as the Messiah and sets out to follow him on the Way. The path that Jesus has set for us which all can take, returning from their own exile from God. Jesus is called by the Father to be the ultimate high priest who offers the sacrificial blood not of some animal but of himself.

SOME OF us constitutionally resist change of any sort. Some, particularly many younger people, are urgent for change, though even among younger people there is often a real element of conservatism. In the past twenty years, there have been huge changes in the world, in our local society and in the Church. Those of us who are older can sit back over a cup of tea or a pint and think of the 'Good old days'. For younger people the 'Good old days' are history, not reality, and fall under intense criticism and are often seen as 'bad old days' - causing argument and conflict between generations.

As Christians, we are pulled both ways, because Jesus is God, eternal and unchanging, but is God-made-man who comes into human history as a paradox, a contradiction. He proclaims the 'law and the prophets' which will not change - but he introduces radical change. He preaches love, forgiveness, service of God and neighbour, suffering, the love of God expressed in 'Fatherhood'. He dies and rises. He shatters Judaic religion as accepted, by moving from the Old Covenant - the law and the prophets - to the New Covenant - God so loves the world, forgiveness, repentance, the life of the Spirit.

Much as we may resist change, feel uncomfortable with it, and even need to challenge some forms of change, we have a duty to be open, to listen and to move forward. Time waits for no one! We must take up the mantle and follow Jesus. In the gospel today we read that among all the people around it is a blind man called Bartimaeus who sees that Jesus is the Son of David. More than that he realises what Jesus has to offer. He calls Jesus *Rabbuni* which Mark translates as meaning *master;* what it really means is *my master*. He has recognised that Jesus has something to give to him as a person. So what happens when Jesus heals him? He follows Jesus on the Way. We must accept the change in our lives that being a follower of Jesus causes. We must see with a new sight and follow his way.

31st Sunday of the Year

Deuteronomy 6:2-6 Hebrews 7:23-28 Mark 12:28-34

Jesus links the two commandments of love of God and of neighbour into one great law of love. In this love Jesus offered himself as the great once and for all sacrifice for us. Through this sacrifice he constantly intercedes for us to the Father. Those who understand this are close to the kingdom of God.

AS THOUGH to underline the central position in God's revelation to his people in both Old and New Testaments, at various points in the Church's liturgical calendar we have a recurrence of readings referring to the two great commandments. There is something very strengthening about this and it helps, I think, to make sure that among all the other important and varied aspects of the revelation, we do not lose sight of our daily standard of living.

This Sunday in the first reading (*Deuteronomy 6:2-6*), Moses tells the people to fear God all the days of their life and to keep his laws and commandments. And he continues by stating the first great commandment:

> *The Lord our God is the one Lord. You shall love the Lord your God with all your heart, with all your soul, with all your strength.*

In this version, of course, there is no mention of the neighbour, which occurs elsewhere.

When asked in the Gospel (*Mark 12:28-34*) by a scribe 'Which is the first of all the commandments?', Jesus gives a longer version and adds 'and the second is this: 'You must love your neighbour as yourself.' The Scribe applauds and amplifies his answer and Jesus commands him saying: 'You are not far from the Kingdom of God.'

If we can keep those two great commandments close to our hearts and live them out, then we can be sure that we too are not far from the Kingdom of God, which is a joyful support day by day. It helps us to keep our focus beyond our own lives to the needs of others.

So how much are we prepared to love God and neighbour? Are we willing to offer our lives to God and dedicated ourselves to him? As for our neighbour are we willing to reach out and help when they need it? Are we willing to be so caring that we are always trying to anticipate their needs? Well are we?

32nd Sunday of the Year

1 Kings 17:10-16 Hebrews 9:24-28 Mark 12:38-44

In the Bible the widow is shown as needing and lowly. God loves the lowly as the ones who are most open to the call of faith. The faith that is ready to believe that through Christ there is real redemption and an answer to the world's distress. There is, because once he offered his life on the cross.

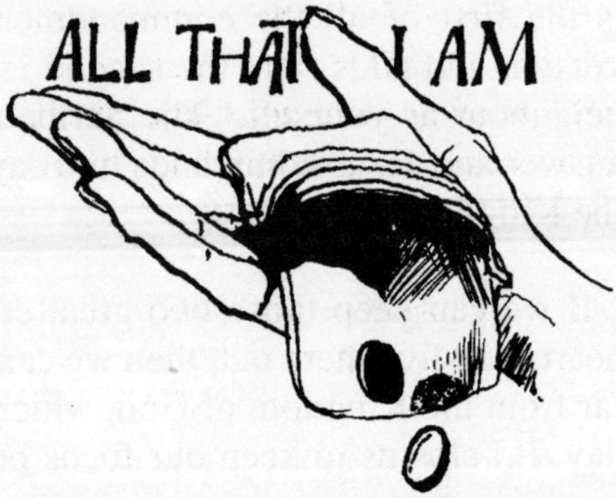

WHEN JESUS was living his few years of preaching and teaching in Palestine, he did a great deal of healing - he went about healing. If you read about these miracles, you will find time and again that he says words like 'Your Faith has made you whole'. 'Faith is the foundation of things hoped for', writes St. Paul. Oddly enough, some cures seem to come to those who apparently have no faith! But when we come, we come to pray in faith, knowing the love of God.

The Lord has said in the Gospel 'Come to me all you who labour and are heavy burdened'. Anyone who is sick is both 'labouring' and also 'heavy burdened'. It does not matter whether it is toothache, migraine, arthritis, blindness, depression, loss of hearing or old age. Each of us who has a 'health burden' should try to link 'cure' or living-with-pain-and-disability into prayer and faith. Sadly it is easy to behave as though there is nothing that can be done! 'Grin and bear it' is a very British motto! But Jesus makes the offer - 'come to me'. At least give him the chance - come to him and ask seriously, earnestly, deeply for what you want and need from his healing hands and heart. I personally have come across the most wonderful 'cures'.

For myself, the Lord did nothing for the arthritis which crippled me. In addition to prayer, trying acupuncture and 'grinning and bearing it', I had to turn to the surgeon and have a hip replacement. From my point of view, the work of the surgeon, anaesthetist and nurses was a miracle of human skill, patience and caring. But I was also very conscious of being upheld by the prayers of so many of you. I urge you to be always aware of the need to pray for and serve the suffering and the dying. Support in suffering is enormously important from family, friends, professionals and parish community members. The Lord talks of giving a cup of cold water as a memorable act in God's sight. We really have the opportunity to give much more than a cup of cold water! As we pray for healing, let us ask ourselves in what practical way - in prayer or service -we are contributing to the healing of our friends, neighbours and community.

33rd Sunday of the Year

Daniel 12:1-13 Hebrews 10:11-14,18 Mark 13:24-32

With the coming of the Christ the final days have begun. We who wait for the second coming should make ourselves ready. It is useless to think about the date and the time of this for it is only those who share the faith of the Lord who will be also share his glory. We should live a life that is always ready for this wonderful event.

MOST PEOPLE - young, middling or elderly will have had the experience of being depressed. We all have moods - laughter and tears, sorrows and joys, on top of the world - or depressed. Often these moods vary considerably even within one day. I can get up in the morning with a sore head, and then find by evening I am the life and soul of the party! Depression is not the same. This is an awful state which seizes a person. It is like going into a fog or a long dark tunnel with no escape. Generally there is no glimmer of light, no way out. It does not help if someone says ‘Snap out of it’. We have to live through and with depression if it takes us: we need a lot of kindness and patience from others: there are no easy solutions. It does help to cling to God, to talk to someone understanding, to be about with people.

Feast of Christ The King

Daniel 7:13-14 Apocalypse 1:5-8 John 18:33-37

The kingdom of Jesus is not of this world, yet he is the just judge of this world. His glory is shown not on a throne but the cross. The paradox before us is that by being lifted up on the cross and shedding his blood he has become the saviour and redeemer of all. Through his love we are one with God.

THIS WEEKEND - the last weekend of the Church's liturgical year - we celebrate the Feast of Christ the King. The preface of the Mass for the day says:

As king he claims dominion over all creation that he may present to you, his almighty Father, an eternal and universal kingdom: a kingdom of truth and life, a kingdom of holiness and grace, a kingdom of justice, love & peace.

Our first duty and joy, then, is to proclaim that 'Our Lord reigns' - in our minds, in our hearts, in our lives. But what does that mean? How does he reign? Firstly, by faith. Unless we believe in him, there can be no loyalty, no desire to discover and follow his will. So - do you *really* believe in God and Jesus his Son?

No? - well then - face that negative and decide not just to pay lip-service to a belief you do not have, which is dishonest and undermines true belief.

Yes? Well then, live out your belief by being seen and known to be an active Catholic. Do not hide your light - Christ's light - under anything. Walk tall and be proud to be a sister or brother of Christ. Of course, some of the things which Christ teaches and tells us to teach are hard, uncompromising and difficult to put across in this modern world - even difficult for us to accept and believe ourselves. So - we are challenged - believe - be loyal - be a witness. And the witness is to truth and life - to holiness and grace, to justice, love and peace. It is quite a task - will you take it on more enthusiastically from today? This is especially an important challenge to young people, because this is a day dedicated to youth. However - much as I want to share with youth, with young people, it is important young people think and work out what is their reaction to 'Our God Reigns'.

Corpus Christi

Exodus 24:3-8 Hebrews 9:11-15 Mark 14:12-16,22-26

In the Old Testament the blood of animals was offered as an atonement for the sins of the people when they moved away from the Covenant given by Moses. In Christ's blood we have a new Covenant that is given once and for all as the perfect sacrifice.

CORPUS CHRISTI comes as one of a series of major celebrations following the resurrection. We first have the Ascension which leads on to Pentecost and Trinity Sunday. Then there is Corpus Christi and St. Peter and St. Paul.

Corpus Christi was not a very early feast and was really established to re-emphasise the reality of the presence of Jesus in his body and blood under the appearance of bread and wine. This is, after all, a mystery. Neither the priest nor any member of the congregation can *see* any change or difference in the bread and the wine after the words of consecration. Each time the priest says the words, he says them *in* faith. Each time he calls *on* the people to proclaim the mystery - it is the mystery *OF FAITH*. So you and I are asked to be humbly present and to call on our personal faith and the faith of the Church to acknowledge what we can only believe by faith.

The Corpus Christi celebration itself has led on to different ways of honouring and devoting ourselves to the presence of Christ in the Blessed Sacrament. There has been much joyous institution of processions carrying the Blessed Sacrament inside and outside Churches. Adoration of the Blessed Sacrament through exposition on the altar, sometimes day and night in particular Churches, has had a large popularity and I am glad to say this particular devotion now seems to be blossoming.

Given such a tremendous gift, we should value it and treasure it in our prayer and devotion.

St. Peter and St. Paul

Acts 12:1-11 2 Timothy 4:6-8,17-18 Matthew 16:13-19

By their deaths in Rome these two great saints have been linked in the eyes of the Church. Yet they are very different people. Peter the impetuous fisherman and Paul the proud tentmaker. Through their leadership the Church was able to consolidate in the very heart of the pagan empire.

THE FEAST of St. Peter and St. Paul is always seen as a great feast of the Church which in so many ways owes its growth and development to their writings and leadership. In earlier days, before the liturgy changes of Vatican II, it always seemed as though 29th June was really honouring St. Peter, and St. Paul had a follow-up feast on 30th June. This is now different and we can honour both on the one day.

It remains true that the two are very different characters, had very different origins in Israel and very different summonses by Jesus Christ. Simon, a fisherman, is first told of Jesus by Andrew who comes to him after spending a day with John in Jesus' company. 'We have found the Messiah' Andrew declares. But then Jesus himself calls Simon from his nets and names him Peter, the rock on which he will build his Church. Thenceforth, Peter, a most endearing character, shows his impetuosity, his total commitment, his weakness and denial, his repentance and reinstatement in love and service - and finally his leadership and ultimate humility in dying for Christ.

Peter is such a wonderful character and so utterly human, his character deserves from us a deeper insight through study of him in Scripture and the early life of the Church and in meditation on him. He should be very important, very uplifting and very consoling in our own attempts to stay close to Jesus and his Church.

The strong, fiery, learned and crusading character of Saul, who also had his name changed to Paul, is a contrast to Peter and also furnishes a teaching which gives a very strong and even dominant line to guide and lead the Church. Both his preaching and his writing are of immense importance in the whole life of the Church. Like Peter, only in a way more so, he should hold our attention and take our time in prayer and study of him and his teaching. We need the guidance of the Spirit and much time to attempt to plumb his depth.

Feast of the Transfiguration

Daniel 7:9-10,13-14   2 Peter 1:16-19   Mark 9:2-10

In the wanderings in the desert the tent or Tabernacle became a symbol of the people's nearness to God. When Christ is revealed in his glory Peter can only think of making tents. A recognition that they were truly in the presence of the divine.

ON THIS feast, the second reading is from St. Peter (*2 Peter 1:16-19*). It is rather beautiful, because he uses his own personal experience as a basic grounding for his preaching: he says it is not cleverly invented myths when he brought the knowledge of the power and coming of Jesus Christ: 'We had seen his majesty for ourselves' ... the sublime glory itself spoke to him and said 'This is my son, the Beloved: he enjoys my favour.' It is always very powerful to be an eyewitness and by the time he wrote his second letter, he had experienced so much more.

The Gospel tells us of the actual happening. *Mark 9:2-10* was not there. It is clear that the disciples had a mixture of emotions including wonder, fear and so on. Then there was the cloud and the voice from a cloud which covered them saying: 'This is my son, the Beloved. Listen to him.' And finally only Jesus was there.

It is interesting that Peter's reaction was to build three tents, and the voice rather suppressed this and simply told them to listen. But when Jesus talked to them, he told them to say nothing of what they had seen 'until after the Son of Man had risen from the dead'. They obeyed him but clearly could not fathom what 'rising from the dead' could mean. Of course, by the time he wrote his letter, Peter had experienced the death of Jesus and also the extraordinary event of his rising from the dead.

Till the next life, we will not experience Jesus rising in quite the same way as Peter, but we can deepen our understanding in prayer.

Jesus took Peter, James and John up a mountain and prayed there, shining in transfiguring glory. Moses and Elijah appeared with him and the disciples got very afraid - but a voice from Heaven said 'This is my beloved Son. Listen to him'. And they then saw only Jesus. This revelation was kept to the three, Peter, James and John. At that time they were given an insight, as later Paul talks of being taken up into heaven to see things normally hidden. I think it is important to get two insights ourselves from this transfiguration.

- Jesus *is* both God and Man. In this world, the main part of his life was not 'in glory' but in the ordinary taking up of his cross daily. After this experience, he and Peter, James and John went down the mountain with their 'secret' and found the other apostles struggling ineffectually to effect a cure. Jesus' message was the hard one - Prayer and Fasting.

- Prayer is essential for each and all. But the revelations and insights are not necessarily for all. Some seem to have wonderful insights and a sense of closeness in Jesus. Some simply seem to struggle on. Both are on the path of love to God if they persevere in prayer. And a 'revelation' or insight you may receive personally.

Assumption of Our Lady

Apocalypse 11:19:12:1-6,10   1 Corinthians 15:20-26   Luke 1:39-56

Filled with joy Mary is moved to give praise to God for the great things he has done for her. She shows us that his mercy lasts from age to age and that he will exalt those who are downtrodden. It is through this mercy given to us by Christ that we are saved and live as part of the kingdom.

The Feast of the Assumption of Our Lady falls in the middle of what is traditionally the summer holidays in much of the Western World. This is certainly true in Europe, where I write. The result is that in England, where it is a holiday of obligation, it tends to be something of a nuisance, especially if the family is staying away and have to find Mass times. Often it is simply forgotten.

The readings are the same for each year in the three year cycle. Without repetition, it is not easy to write anything different year by year. But is it necessary to be 'different'? The Church in her wisdom gives us the same liturgical cycle, though much of the time she varies the scriptural texts. I suspect it is good for us in the holiday season to come back to a well-known feast. Then, if we do miss the actual day, we can recall the theme of the feast and meditate on it in our own way. Personally, I come back

again and again to two things - one is the idea of the falling asleep of the Virgin. After her life of continual presence with Jesus, a faithful, generally silent presence, and one shot through with anxiety, pain and grief, especially at the Passion and death of Jesus - after all this, Mary thoroughly deserved to die in the peace of the Lord, a true falling asleep in love. And the other, Mary's injunction at Cana - the very simple, very direct command to the steward at the feast 'Do whatever he tells you'. That is what Mary did! Would that we could do the same throughout our lives and so be ready, when he calls, to fall asleep in the love of the Lord.

All Saints

Apocalypse 7:2-4;9-14 1 John 3:1-3 Matthew 5:1-12

The saints are our example. They are the members of the people of God whose lives shine out as true followers of Christ. They have lived the Beatitudes and therefore are true children of God.

TODAY WE celebrate All Saints. We include all those whom the Church has herself recognised as Saints from John the Baptist, through the Apostles and martyrs to a whole host whose names we know and whose feasts are marked by the Church, though not all are celebrated universally, and the very authenticity of some is doubtful.

This known catalogue forms a varied pattern of example in style of life, ways of prayer and particular charisms that each one has. Much richness and witness flows to us from studying their lives and spirituality. It is possible that each individual person may have one or more saint whose life, example or teaching seems particularly apt and appealing for him or her. We also, of course, are many of us *named* after a saint, which gives an immediate affinity. Indeed in many countries it is a person's 'Saints' day' that is celebrated rather than a birthday.

The first reading of this feast is from the Apocalypse where John sees 'a huge number, impossible to count, of people from every nation, race, tribe and language'. This should underline for us that it is not only the well-known saints we are honouring, but also that vast crowd who have been converging on God's heavenly Kingdom ever since creation. Alleluia! Praise God and the Lord for them.

And finally, we should not forget that the early writings refer to all those belonging to the Church as saints. You and I are included in that number as we strive to live by Christ's law and the Sacraments in his Church.

ABBA, FATHER

Christian unity

THIS WEEK we concentrate on Christian Unity. Each of us should ask ourselves where we stand, how we work and whether we pray for Christian Unity. Our understanding is that Jesus really wanted and prayed for unity. In his day, as a Jew, he already knew the deep divisions there were among the various groupings in Israel, and he was himself setting a new trend. Jesus, of course, was never a Christian! It was his followers who came to be called Christian at a later stage. He was a Jew all through his life and through his death.

Within the early Church, there soon also started to be factions - 'I'm for Paul, I'm for Apollo' and so on. Very soon there were wide differences, leading to the early Councils of the Church, which were called to clarify the belief of Christians and to condemn heresies and heretics. Not infrequently, we in these islands date every split in unity to the Reformation period. This is not true at all - among other things, the whole Orthodox body of believers came away centuries before Luther, Calvin, Zwingli and others. But today, much work has been done on the higher theological level with the Anglican/Roman Catholic International Commission (ARCIC) which had its origins back in 1967. Since then the Commission has issued documents on Ministry, Eucharist and Authority. A new series of discussions are under way at the moment as ARCIC II. But it is also important that at a lower level, in our parochial and local community situation, we should try to discover each other, our similarities and differences.

For many people, it seems difficult enough to try to live and pray and worship in our own Roman Catholic teaching and sacraments, without trying to understand and live with the differing emphasis, custom and even teaching of Anglicans, Methodists, Baptists and other Christians. Certainly there is much to be done to deepen our faith, our prayer life, our sharing in Mass, the sacraments and the charitable works of the parish, diocese and world Church. However, I suggest that, if we do get closer and deeper into relation with Jesus - we will be more likely to follow St. Paul's command: 'Make your own the mind of Christ' *(Philippians 2:5)*. And it was Jesus who prayed 'may they all be one, just as, Father, you are in me and I am in you, so that they also may be in us, so that the world may believe it was you who sent me.' *(John 17:21)*. So I urge you this week and this year:

- To accept and do something personal and positive about deepening your own Christian living.

- To encourage in yourself the desire to pray, to serve others, to worship God at Mass and in the Sacraments.

- To live in constructive peace with your neighbours and to work for Unity among Christians.

- To foster greater understanding with those of other faiths does not guarantee your perseverance.

Index

General

H

I

J

K

L

M

N